☑ P9-EMG-448

CRITICAL ACCLAIM FOR *TO BE A SLAVE*

A Newbery Honor Book
An ALA Notable Children's Book
School Library Journal Best Book of the Year
Horn Book Fanfare Honor List
Lewis Carroll Shelf Award
New York Times Outstanding Book of the Year

"From history—and for our time—there's nothing better than Julius Lester's *To Be a Slave*, which offers the eloquent personal testimony of those who wore the shackles, had their flesh ripped by the lash, and suffered the most sickening outrages."
—*The New York Times Book Review*

"This is how it was—a powerful chronicle of tragedy skillfully assembled from the eloquent slaves themselves, accompanied by pointed but unobtrusive editorial commentary and starkly dramatic illustrations."
—*School Library Journal*

Also from **Point** by Julius Lester:
This Strange New Feeling

point

TO BE A SLAVE

Julius Lester

Illustrated by
Tom Feelings

SCHOLASTIC INC.
New York Toronto London Auckland Sydney

ISBN 0-590-42460-2

Text copyright © 1968 by Julius Lester. Illustrations copyright © 1968 by Tom Feelings. All rights reserved. This edition published by Scholastic Inc., 730 Broadway, New York, NY 10003, by arrangement with Dial Books for Young Readers, a division of E. P. Dutton, Inc., POINT is a trademark of Scholastic Inc.

48 47 46 45 44 43 42 41 40 39 38 37   4 5 6 7 8/0

The ancestry of any black American can be traced to
a bill of sale and no further. In many instances even that
cannot be done. Such is true of part of my family.

This book is dedicated to the memory of my great-grandparents:

Elvira Smith
Maggie Carson
Slaves in Arkansas
and
Square and Angeline Lester
Austin and Sylvia Jones
Slaves in Mississippi
and
to those whose names are now
unknown.

I never knew them,
but I am proud to be one of their descendants.
I hope that I may be worthy of them, their strength,
and their courage.

CONTENTS

"In all the books that you have studied you never have studied Negro history, have you? You studied about the Indian and white folks, but what did they tell you about the Negro? If you want Negro history, you will have to get it from somebody who wore the shoe, and by and by from one to the other, you will get a book."

———EX-SLAVE,
Tennessee

NOTE

One of the greatest overlooked sources for information concerning slavery has been the words of those who were slaves. During the first half of the nineteenth century the American Anti-Slavery Society and other northern abolition groups took down the stories of thousands of blacks who escaped from the South. The narratives of ex-slaves became a literary genre in the period before the Civil War, and these narratives became a potent weapon in the battle to sway northern public opinion against slavery.

After the Civil War, interest in the stories of ex-slaves dwindled until the 1930's. It was then that the Federal Writers' Project was organized, and one task it undertook was to interview those ex-slaves still alive. At least two books were published using this material: B. A. Botkin's *Lay My Burden Down* and the Federal Writers' Project book, *The Negro in Virginia*. But most of the material remains unpublished.

In the spring of 1963 I learned that all of the slave narratives taken down by the Federal Writers' Project were stored at the Archive of Folksong at the Library of Congress. I spent several weeks reading through the over six thousand pages of manuscripts. I wish to express my thanks to Mrs. Rae Korson and Mr. Joe Hickerson of the Archive of Folksong for their kind assistance to me.

The nineteenth-century slave narratives and those taken down by the Federal Writers' Project differ in one important respect. The Federal Writers' Project was as interested in preserving the speech patterns and language of the ex-slaves as it was in gathering information about slavery. Therefore the interviews were taken down word-for-word. The nineteenth-century slave narratives were taken down by white abolitionists in many instances and then rewritten by them to conform to the literary standards of the time. Also, many abolitionists felt that to publish the narratives in the language of the ex-slaves—a language that had its own rules of grammar and pronunciation—would give the enemies of the abolitionist cause ammunition for their arguments of black inferiority. Thus great pains were taken to present the stories in a manner that could not be criticized. There is no reason to believe, however, that because these narratives were made to conform to certain literary standards that they are not reflective of the thoughts and experiences of those who endured slavery.

In this book the reader will find numerous examples of both kinds of narratives. Those of the Federal

Writers' Project offer the advantage of an earthy directness of communication. The nineteenth-century narratives offer the advantage of analysis of the slave experience. Together the two present a vivid picture of how the slaves felt about slavery.

I have taken the liberty of modernizing punctuation, as well as the dialect spellings which were the attempts of white writers to record Negro speech. This was done for the sole purpose of making the material more readable.

The sources of quoted material are indicated beneath each passage. The first line is the name of the ex-slave speaking, if the name is known. The second indicates the source of the material by author's name. In four instances there is no author. These are the narrative material taken from the Fisk University collection of slave narratives, the Library of Congress, the transcript of the hearings held by the House of Commons on the slave trade in 1790 and 1791, and from *The Negro in Virginia*. Extracts from these are indicated by Fisk, Library of Congress, *Evidence on the Slave Trade*, and *The Negro in Virginia*. Full information on sources can be found in the bibliography.

JULIUS LESTER
April 11, 1968

PROLOGUE

About the latter end of August, a Dutch man of Warr
of the burden of a 160 tunes arrived at Point Comfort,
the commanders name Capt. Jope, his pilott for the West
Indyes one Mr. Marmaduke an Englishman. They mett
with the Trer in the West Indyes, and determyned to hold
consort shipp hetherward, but in their passage lost one
the other. He brought not anything but 20 and odd Negroes, which the Governor and Cape Marchant bought for
victualle (whereof he was in great need as he ptended)
at the best and easiest rates they could. . . .

Letter from John Rolfe of the Jamestown, Virginia, Colony
to Sir Edwin Sandys, Treasurer of the Virginia Company
of London. *The Negro in Virginia*, p. 1.

*The African slave trade was already over a hundred
years old when the Dutch ship landed twenty Africans
at the Jamestown colony in 1619. Portugal had introduced Africans to Europe in the early sixteenth century.*

The slave trade soon extended into England and Spain and to their colonies in the New World of the Americas when it was discovered. Africans accompanied Spanish explorers on their journeys to the New World. There were thirty blacks with Balboa when he discovered the Pacific Ocean; blacks accompanied Pizarro to Peru, Coronado to New Mexico, Narvaez and Cabeza de Vaca in their explorations of what is now Arizona and New Mexico. Blacks also accompanied the French explorers to Canada and the Mississippi River valley. Thus blacks were a part of the New World long before the Mayflower, even before the settling of Jamestown in 1609.

Yet even with the existence of a slave trade and the early presence of blacks in what was to become the United States, slavery was not introduced immediately. The English colonists were in great need of labor to help settle their new colonies. At first they tried to use the Indians. This proved impossible. The Indians came from a society and a way of life that was relatively uncomplicated. This background did not prepare them for the disciplined and complex way of life and work necessary for the plantation system. They also proved to be very susceptible to the diseases of the colonists. Everywhere Indian labor was used, it proved to be highly unsuccessful.

England then tried sending poor whites, prisoners, and debtors from England and Ireland to the American colonies. Men, women, and children were often kidnapped and sent to America to work. These whites were *held as indentured servants for seven years and then released. This soon created the need for a continual supply of people to work. Another disadvantage was simply the fact that a white indentured servant could run away, and because he was white, he could go to another place, change his name, and have no fear of being caught.*

Gradually the English colonists turned to Africans as the ideal solution. Because they were black, it would be difficult for them to run away and escape detection. Too, they could be bought outright and held for as long as they lived. And finally, the supply was inexhaustible.

Eighteen years after the first Africans came to the Jamestown colony, the first American-built slave ship sailed from Marblehead, Massachusetts. Its name was the Desire. *The slave ships sailed to the west coast of Africa, and there the captains of the slave vessels went about their job of loading the ships with blacks to bring to America.*

Granny Judith said that in Africa they had very few pretty things, and that they had no red colors in cloth. In fact, they had no cloth at all. Some strangers with pale faces come one day and dropped a small piece of red flannel down on the ground. All the black folks grabbed for it. Then a larger piece was dropped a little further on, and on until the river was reached. Then a large piece was dropped in the river and on the other side. They was led on, each one trying to get a piece as it was dropped.

Finally, when the ship was reached, they dropped large pieces on the plank and up into the ship till they got as many blacks on board as they wanted. Then the gate was chained up and they could not get back. That is the way Granny Judith say they got her to America.

RICHARD JONES
Botkin, p. 57.

The capture of Africans was usually much more difficult than this. When the slave trade began, West Africa had a highly developed civilization, with complex economic and political institutions. It was because of their sophisticated civilization that they could be used so easily in the rapidly growing economy of America.

Generally the slave trade was carried out in one of three ways. The first and easiest was simply to lie in wait until somebody came by, and then capture him. This method soon gave way to an alliance between white slave traders and black African tribal chiefs. The African chief would make war on another tribe for the purpose of capturing as many people as possible. He would turn them over to the white slave traders in exchange for various items the chief wanted—tobacco, guns, ammunition, liquor. This arrangement evolved into a more complicated one in which one African chief would align with another chief, who would agree to sell some of his own tribesmen or others he had captured in a battle. He would be paid in goods for these soon-to-be slaves by the first African chief, who in turn would sell them to a white slave trader.

Charles Ball, a slave during the early nineteenth century, came into contact with many Africans who had been brought to America. His own grandfather had come from Africa, and as a child Ball had heard many stories about Africa from him. In his autobiography he recorded the story of one slave who was brought from Africa to America.

. . . we were alarmed one morning, just at the break of day, by the horrible uproar caused by mingled shouts of men, and blows given with heavy sticks, upon large wooden drums. The village was surrounded by enemies, who attacked us with clubs, long wooden spears, and bows and arrows. After fighting for more than an hour, those who were not fortunate enough to run away were made prisoners. It was not the object of our enemies to kill; they wished to take us alive and sell us as slaves. I was knocked down by a heavy blow of a club, and when I recovered from the stupor that followed, I found myself tied fast with the long rope I had brought from the desert. . . .

We were immediately led away from this village, through the forest, and were compelled to travel all day as fast as we could walk. . . . We traveled three weeks in the woods—sometimes without any path at all—and arrived one day at a large river with a rapid current. Here we were forced to help our conquerors to roll a great number of dead trees into the water from a vast pile that had been thrown together by high floods.

These trees, being dry and light, floated high out of the water; and when several of them were fastened together with the tough branches of young trees, [they] formed a raft, upon which we all placed ourselves, and descended the river for three days, when we came in sight of what appeared to me the most wonderful object in the world; this was a large ship at anchor in the river. When our raft came near the ship, the white people—for such they were on board—assisted to take us on the deck, and the logs were suffered to float down the river.

I had never seen white people before and they appeared to me the ugliest creatures in the world. The persons who brought us down the river received payment for us of the people in the ship, in various articles, of which I remember that a keg of liquor, and some yards of blue and red cotton cloth were the principal.

Ball, pp. 158–159.

Once on board, the slaves were taken below the deck and chained together in what was called the slave galley. It was here that they were kept throughout the long voyage from Africa to America. And it was here that millions died from the conditions on board the ship.

. . . he [the ship's doctor] made the most of the room, and *wedged them in.* They had not so much room *as a man in his coffin,* either in length or breadth. It was impossible for them to turn or shift with any degree of ease. He had often occasion to go from one side of their room to the other, in which case he always *took off his shoes,* but could not avoid pinching them; he has the marks on his feet where they bit and scratched him. In every voyage when the ship was full they complained of heat and want of air. Confinement in this situation was so injurious that he has known them *go down apparently in good health at night and found dead in the morning.* On his last voyage he opened a stout man who so died. He found the contents of the thorax and abdomen healthy, and therefore concludes *he died of suffocation in the night.*

Evidence on the Slave Trade, p. 47.

Others died because they took their own lives rather than live as slaves.

At the time we came into this ship, she was full of black people, who were all confined in a dark and low place, in irons. The women were in irons as well as the men.

About twenty persons were seized in our village at the time I was; and amongst these were three children so young that they were not able to walk or to eat any hard substance. The mothers of these children had brought them all the way with them and had them in their arms when we were taken on board this ship.

When they put us in irons to be sent to our place of confinement in the ship, the men who fastened the irons on these mothers took the children out of their hands and threw them over the side of the ship into the water. When this was done, two of the women leaped overboard after the children—the third was already confined by a chain to another woman and could not get into the water, but in struggling to disengage herself, she broke her arm and died a few days after of a fever. One of the two women who were in the river was carried down by the weight of her irons before she could be rescued; but the other was taken up by some men in a boat and brought on board. This woman threw herself overboard one night when we were at sea.

The weather was very hot whilst we lay in the river and many of us died every day; but the number brought on board greatly exceeded those who died, and at the end of two weeks, the place in which we were confined was so full that no one could lie down; and we were obliged to sit all the time, for the room was not high enough for us to stand. When our prison could hold no more, the ship sailed down the river; and on the night of the second day after she sailed, I heard the roaring of the ocean as it dashed against her sides.

After we had been at sea some days, the irons were removed from the women and they were permitted to go upon deck; but whenever the wind blew high, they were driven down amongst us.

We had nothing to eat but yams, which were thrown amongst us at random—and of these we had scarcely enough to support life. More than one third of us died on the passage and when we arrived at Charleston, I was not able to stand. It was more than a week after I left the ship before I could straighten my limbs. I was bought by a trader with several others, brought up the country and sold to my present master. I have been here five years.

Ball, pp. 159–160.

. . . the man had not taken his food and refused taking any. Mild means were then used to divert him from his resolution, as well as promises that he should have anything he wished for; but he still refused to eat. They then whipped him with the cat, but this also was ineffectual. He always kept his teeth so fast that it was impossible to get anything down. . . . In this state he was four or five days, when he was brought up as dead to be thrown overboard; but Mr. Wilson, finding life still existing, repeated his endeavours though in vain, and two days afterwards he was brought up again in the same state as before. He then seemed to wish to get up. The crew assisted him and brought him aft to the fireplace, when in a feeble voice in his own tongue he asked for water, which was given him. Upon this they began to have hopes of dissuading him from his design, but he again shut his teeth as fast as ever, *and resolved to die,* and on the ninth day from his first refusal he died.

Evidence on the Slave Trade, p. 52.

It is estimated that some fifty million people were taken from the continent during the years of the slave trade. These fifty million were, of course, the youngest, the strongest, those most capable of bringing great profit, first to the slave trader, and later to the slave owner. These Africans were scattered throughout South America, the islands of the West Indies, and the United States. Africa's citizens became the laboring backbone of much of the western hemisphere.

Slavery differed from country to country. But it was in The United States that a system of slavery evolved that was more cruel and total than almost any other system of slavery devised by one group of men against another. No other country where blacks were enslaved destroyed African culture to the extent that it was destroyed here. Today there still exist, in South America and the Caribbean Islands, African religions, music, and language, which came over on the slave ships. Only fragments of Africa remain among the blacks of the United States.

The slavery instituted by the founders of America has few comparisons for its far-reaching cruelty.

· 1 ·

TO BE A SLAVE

To be a slave. To be owned by another person, as a car, house, or table is owned. To live as a piece of property that could be sold—a child sold from its mother, a wife from her husband. To be considered not human, but a "thing" that plowed the fields, cut the wood, cooked the food, nursed another's child; a "thing" whose sole function was determined by the one who owned you.

To be a slave. To know, despite the suffering and deprivation, that you were human, more human than he who said you were not human. To know joy, laughter, sorrow, and tears and yet be considered only the equal of a table.

To be a slave was to be a human being under conditions in which that humanity was denied. They were not slaves. They were people. Their condition was slavery.

They who were held as slaves looked upon themselves and the servitude in which they found themselves with the eyes and minds of human beings, conscious of everything that happened to them, conscious of all that went on around them. Yet slaves are often pictured as little more than dumb, brute animals, whose sole attributes were found in working, singing, and dancing. They were like children and slavery was actually a benefit to them—this was the view of those who were not slaves. Those who were slaves tell a different story.

Now that slavery is over, I don't want to be in nary 'nother slavery, and if ever nary 'nother come up, I wouldn't stay here.

SALLY CARDER
Library of Congress

One day I saw the foreman slap a nigger for drinking at the dipper too long. The nigger picked up a shovel and slam him in the head and run. Back in the slavery days they didn't do something and run. They run before they did it, 'cause they knew that if they struck a white man, there wasn't going to be a nigger. In them days, they run to keep from doing something. Nowadays they do it and then they run.

ANONYMOUS
Library of Congress

We didn't know nothing like young folks do now. We hardly knowed our names. We was cussed for so many bitches and sons of bitches and bloody bitches and blood of bitches. We never heard our names scarcely at all. First young man I went with wanted to know my initials!

What did I know 'bout initials? You ask 'em ten years old now and they'll tell you. That was after the war. Initials!!!

SALLIE CRANE
Library of Congress

You want to know what they did in slavery times. They were doing just what they do now. The white folks was beating the niggers, burnin' 'em and boilin' 'em, workin' 'em and doin' any other thing they wanted to do with them.

ALICE JOHNSON
Library of Congress

I was here in slavery days. I was here. When I come here, colored people didn't have their ages. The boss man had it.

ANONYMOUS
Library of Congress

They knew, and when given the opportunity, they would talk of slavery in vivid, fresh, and alive language. They had no formal education, but they had the education of day-to-day living, of observing people and nature, for their lives depended on such knowledge.

Not all slaves had the same experiences. A few were so enslaved that once slavery ended, they were sorry.

I wants to see old Master again anyways. I reckon maybe I'll just go up and ask him what he wants me to do, and he'll tell me, and if I don't know how, he'll show me how, and I'll try to do it to please him. And when I get it done, I want to hear him grumble like he used to and say, "Charley, you ain't got no sense, but you is a good boy. This here ain't very good, but it'll do, I reckon. Get yourself a little piece of that brown sugar, but don't let no niggers see you eating it. If you do, I'll whup your black behind!" That ain't the way it's going to be in Heaven, I reckon, but I can't sit here and think of no way I'd better like to have it.

CHARLEY WILLIAMS
Botkin, p. 110.

The few slaves like this were usually those who worked in the slave owner's house. Charley Williams's relationship with his owner was a perverted one and is an example of the kind of pathetic relationships and people that could exist under slavery.

There were some slaves whose owners were their real fathers. Many of these owners would not acknowledge their slave children. Others would and provided that these, their slave children, were to be freed and sent to school upon the master's death. One unusual slave owner went so far as to educate his black son against slavery.

My master's name was Powhatan Mitchell and he lived at Perch, Virginia, right at the mouth of Peddler River. At that time ol' Master had a ferryboat and three farms. He was a Whig who owned slaves, but was against slavery.

He took me on his knee when I was about three and a half years old, and gave me his birthright. He called up an old sow that had thirteen pigs all different colors. He said, "You see them pigs there? They are all different colors, but all have the same mother and all are brothers and sisters." Then he called up his son and said, "This boy is your brother. I am the daddy of you both. You are to call me Papa henceforth. You are to call this brother of yours, not master, but brother. Never call no white man master. For all are brothers and equal. Black is as good as white. So always keep courage and never back off from a white man. Treat all men alike and call all girls Miss, white and black; but call all men just what they call you. Always be honest and just and upright before all men. When you finish a day's work, get money for it and never take provisions or chattel. If you need provisions or chattel, get the money and buy them." From that day to this I called ol' Master, Papa. I followed his instructions. I have always been honest, just and have contended for what was rightfully mine. I have never feared no man, white nor black.

BYRL ANDERSON
Library of Congress

The typical slave experience, however, was very different and was characterized by a vicious cruelty. Slaves were whipped for the most trifling incidents, and the whip was as often wielded by the slave owner's wife as the slave owner himself.

Whippings were also administered by the plantation overseer, a poor white, who was hired to watch the slaves while they worked, to make sure that they weren't lazy about the work and didn't try to run away. On the larger plantations a trusted slave would help the overseer. Known as the driver, he was used often by the owner or the overseer to give whippings. Sometimes a slave preferred to be whipped by the slave owner, because the driver would be more severe. Other drivers were more lenient.

They whipped my father 'cause he looked at a slave they killed and cried.

ROBERTA MANSON
Library of Congress

One day while my mammy was washing her back my sister noticed ugly disfiguring scars on it. Inquiring about them, we found, much to our amazement, that they were Mammy's relics of the now gone, if not forgotten, slave days. This was her first reference to her "misery days" that she had made in my presence. Of course we all thought she was telling us a big story and we made fun of her. With eyes flashing, she stopped bathing, dried her back and reached for the smelly ol' black whip that hung behind the kitchen door. Bidding us to strip down to our waists, my little mammy with the boney bent-over back, struck each of us as hard as ever she could with that black-snake whip. Each

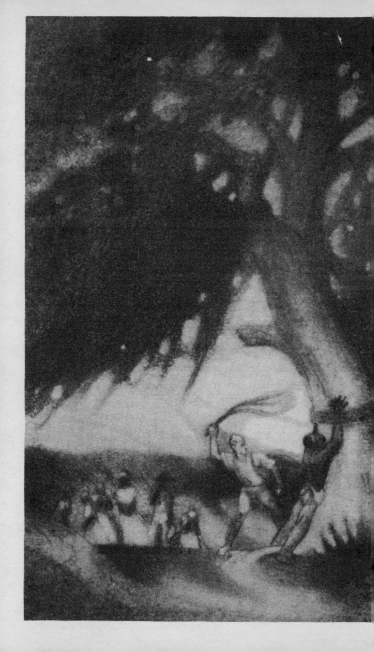

stroke of the whip drew blood from our backs. "Now," she said to us, "you have a taste of slavery days."

FRANK COOPER
Library of Congress

Anytime ol' massa got a slave that been cuttin' up or something, he tell Gabe to give that slave a lashin'. Sometime he come down to the barn to watch it, but most time he just set on the porch and listen to the blows. Ol' Gabe didn't like that whipping business, but couldn't help himself. When massa was there, he would lay it on, because he had to. But when ol' massa wasn't, he never would beat them slaves. Would tie the slave up to one post and lash another one. Of course, the slave would scream and yell to satisfy massa, but he wasn't getting no lashing. After while Gabe would come out the barn and ask massa if that was enough. "Sho', that's plenty," say massa. Once ol' Gabe was beating the post so hard and the slave was yelling so that massa call out to Gabe, "Quit beating that nigger, Gabe. What you trying to do? Kill him?" Slave come running out screaming, with berry wine rubbed all over his back and Massa told Gabe if he didn't stop beating his slaves so hard, he gonna git a lashin' himself.

WEST TURNER
The Negro in Virginia, p. 156.

. . . during my eight years experience as a driver, I learned to handle the whip with marvelous dexterity and precision,

To Be a Slave · 35 ·

throwing the lash within a hair's breadth of the back, the
ear, the nose, without, however, touching either of them.
If Epps was observed at a distance, or we had reason to
apprehend he was sneaking somewhere in the vicinity, I
would commence plying the lash vigorously, when, according to arrangement, they would squirm and screech
as if in agony, although not one of them had in fact been
even grazed. Patsey would take occasion, if he made his
appearance presently, to mumble in his hearing some com-
plaints that Platt [Northup's slave name] was lashing them
the whole time, and Uncle Abram, with an appearance of
honesty peculiar to himself, would declare roundly I had
just whipped them worse than General Jackson whipped
the enemy at New Orleans.

Northup, pp. 226–227.

My master used to throw me in a buck and whip me. He
would put my hands together and tie them. Then he would
strip me naked. Then would make me squat down. Then
he would run a stick through behind my knees and in
front of my elbows. My knee was up against my chest.
My hands was tied together just in front of my shins. The
stick between my arms and my knees held me in a squat.
That's what they call a buck. You couldn't stand up and
you couldn't get your feet out. You couldn't do nothing
but just squat there and take what he put on. You couldn't
move no way at all. Just try to. You just fall over on one
side and have to stay there till you were turned over by
him. He would whip me on one side till that was sore

and full of blood and then he would whip me on the other side till that was all tore up. I got a scar big as the place my ol' mistress hit me. She took a bull whip once. The bull whip had a piece of iron in the handle of it—and she got mad. She was so mad she took the whip and hit me over the head with the butt end of it and the blood flew. It ran all down my back and dripped off my heels.

ELLA WILSON
Library of Congress

Because the slaves were considered property, they were often ordered to do things that were not directly related to their work. If they refused, the consequences were meted out, as described above. The story related below was not an uncommon one in the slave South.

The master would make us slaves steal from each of the slave owners. Our master would make us surround a herd of his neighbor's cattle, round them up at night, and make us slaves stay up all night long and kill and skin every one of them critters, salt the skins down in layers in the master's cellar, and put the cattle piled ceiling high in the smokehouse so nobody could identify skinned cattle.

HENRY JOHNSON
Library of Congress

Perhaps the slave's attitude toward slavery is summed up in the last sentence of the following story. It reveals a complete understanding on the part of the narrator of what slavery was all about, and it also reveals the at-

*titude that most slaves had toward death during slavery.
The circumstances of the story are unusual; the moral
of the story, common.*

Blackshear had them take their babies with them to the
field and it was two or three miles from the house to the
field. He didn't want them to lose time walking backward
and forward nursing. They built a long trough like a great
long old cradle and put all these babies in it every morning
when the mother come out to the field. It was set at the
end of the rows under a big cottonwood tree. When they
were at the other end of the row, all at once a cloud no
bigger than a small spot came up and it grew fast, and it
thundered and lightened as if the world were coming to
an end, and the rain just came down in great sheets. And
when it got so they could go to the other end of the field,
that trough was filled with water and every baby in it was
floating round in the water, drowned. They never got nary
a lick of labor and nary a red penny for any of them
babies.

IDA HUTCHINSON
Library of Congress

*To the slaves it was clear that slavery existed for two
reasons: free labor, and the money that was gotten from
the fruits of that free labor and from selling slaves.
"A lick of labor and . . . a red penny." Black men,
black women, and black children were enslaved because
it was profitable to other men.*

THE AUCTION BLOCK

The institution of slavery had no redeeming virtues for the enslaved. Not even that of stability, of at least being kept on one plantation, in one place all of one's life. The slave had no such assurance, and in fact the rule, more than the exception, was that before his life was over, he would live on at least two, and many times, more plantations.

Slave owners generally sold their slaves for several reasons. Quite often the slave owner would find himself in debt, for personal or business reasons, and to free himself from debt, he would sell some of his slaves. Sometimes the slave owner had an unmanageable slave on his plantation, that is, one who would fight back or run away. These were not few and they were either killed or sold, if they didn't escape first.

Some slave owners were in the business of breeding slaves to be sold. This was particularly true in the state of Virginia, an acknowledged slave-breeding state. Even on plantations where slave breeding was not the sole purpose for the plantation's existence, slave owners preferred women who could bear many children. These children became his work force for the next generation. Or, if he preferred, he could sell them as infants or as children and make a reasonable amount of money.

For the slaves, selling was an occasion of deep sorrow. Particularly for a mother, who had to stand by helpless as her children were carried away to an unknown place. Sometimes, a mother would seek to cheat the auction block.

I don't know how old I was when I found myself standing on the toppen part of a high stump with a lot of white folks walking around looking at the little scared boy that was me.

PRINCE BEE
Library of Congress

My mother told me that he owned a woman who was the mother of seven children, and when her babies would get about a year or two of age, he'd sell them and it would break her heart. She never got to keep them. When her fourth baby was born and was about two months old, she just studied all the time about how she would have to give it up, and one day she said, "I just decided I'm not going to let ol' master sell this baby; he just ain't going to do it." She got up and give it something out of a bottle and pretty soon it was dead.

LOU SMITH
Botkin, p. 154.

The selling of slaves was inhuman in itself, but many slave owners did not even have the decency to tell a slave that he was going to be sold.

Half the time a slave didn't know that he was sold till the master'd call him to the Big House and tell him he had a new master.

MINGO WHITE
Library of Congress

Never knew who massa done sold. I remember one morning ol' white man rode up in a buggy and stop by a gal name Lucy that was working in the yard. He say, "Come on. Get in this buggy. I bought you this morning." Then she beg him to let her go tell her baby and husband goodbye, but he say, "Naw! Get in this buggy! Ain't got no time for crying and carrying on." I started crying myself, 'cause I was so scared he was gonna take me, too. But ol' Aunt Cissy, whose child it was, went to massa and told him he was a mean dirty nigger-trader. Ol' massa was sore, but ain't never said nothin' to Aunt Cissy. Then Hendley what was next to the youngest of her seven children got sick and died. Aunt Cissy ain't sorrowed much. She went straight up to ol' massa and shouted in his face, "Praise God! Praise God! My little child is gone to Jesus. That's one child of mine you never gonna sell."

NANCY WILLIAMS
The Negro in Virginia, p. 172.

I said to him, "For God's sake! Have you bought my wife?"
He said he had. When I asked him what she had done,
he said she had done nothing, but that her master wanted
money. He drew out a pistol and said that if I went near
the wagon on which she was, he would shoot me. I asked
for leave to shake hands with her which he refused, but
said I might stand at a distance and talk with her. My
heart was so full that I could say very little. . . . I have
never seen or heard from her from that day to this. I
loved her as I love my life.

MOSES GRANDY
Nichols, p. 20.

*The sale of slaves was generally carried out in one of
two ways. The most informal was the sale of a slave by
one slave owner to another, usually a friend on a neighboring plantation. The more usual method was through
a slave trader, a man whose business was the buying
and selling of slaves. The slave trader was no different
from the cotton merchant, who bought cotton from the
plantations and sold it at a profit. Most traders operated
on a small scale, but the large traders made a handsome
profit from their business. The famous Confederate
general, Nathan Bedford Forrest, was the largest slave
trader in Memphis, Tennessee, during the 1850's and in
one year, made a profit of $96,000. The largest slave-
trading firm was that of Franklin and Armfield. Their
main office was in Alexandria, Virginia, and they had
representatives in New Orleans, Louisiana; Natchez,*

Mississippi; Richmond and Warrenton, Virginia; and Frederick, Baltimore, and Easton, Maryland. By the time they retired from business, each of them had accumulated over half a million dollars.

The slave market was much like today's stock market. Prices fluctuated according to the economic climate and what was happening in the world. When times were good, selling was good. When times were bad, selling was also. One particular event touched off a big rash of selling. That was the election of Abraham Lincoln as President in 1860.

I was about twelve or fourteen years old when I was sold. A Negro trader came along and bought up all the slaves he could and took us to Louisiana. About this time many people sold their slaves because they felt the same thing was going to happen. One side thought the war would come and all the slaves get freed. All that felt this way about it began to sell so as to get the money. There were others that thought that in case of war the South would win. They held what slaves they had and even bought more.

I first found out that something was going to happen one day when I got back with the mail. My master took the paper I brought and after looking at it a minute he turned to mistress and said, "That old Yankee [Lincoln] has got elected and I am going to sell every nigger I got because he is going to free them."

When this news got out among the slaves there was a lot

of disturbance and speculation on who would be the first one. I was a boy then big enough to work. I had a brother named John and a cousin by the name of Brutus. Both of them were sold and about three weeks later, it came my turn. On the day I left home, everything was sad among the slaves. My mother and father sung and prayed over me and told me how to get along in the world. I took my little bundle of clothes—a pair of slips, a shirt and a pair of jeans pants—and went to give my mama my last farewell. I did not see her again until after the war.

I went on into Charleston. The prices usually went up on slaves in the fall of the year. Along in September what was known as nigger-traders started to coming around Charleston which was a great trading post. When selling time came we had to wash up and comb our hair so as to look as good as we could so as to demand a high price. Oh yes, we had to dress up and parade before the white folks until they picked the ones they wanted. I was sold along with a gang of others to a trader and he took us to Louisiana. There, I believe I was sold to the meanest man that God ever put breath in. Out of seventeen of us sold to him, only four of us got back home. Some died; others he killed.

ANONYMOUS
Fisk, pp. 161–163.

The slave trader's job was to sell to the highest bidder, not to see that each slave was sold to a kind master. The slave trader would come to a town with his slaves chained together into what was called a slave coffle. After advertising his presence in the vicinity and the "merchandise" he had to offer, he would hold an auction. Before the formal bidding began, the prospective buyers and curious non-buyers would get an opportunity to examine the "merchandise."

Every first Tuesday slaves were brought in from Virginia and sold on the block. The auctioneer was Cap'n Dorsey. E. M. Cobb was the slave-bringer. They would stand the slaves up on the block and talk about what a fine-looking specimen of black manhood or womanhood they was, tell how healthy they was, look in their mouth and examine their teeth just like they was a horse, and talk about the kind of work they would be fit for and could do.

MORRIS HILLYER
Library of Congress

The slave trader tried to present his "merchandise" so that it would bring the highest price. This meant that the slaves should look well fed, strong, and healthy. Between the time a slave was bought and sold by a trader, his well-being was the responsibility of that trader. Most slave traders wanted to keep their expenses as low as possible so they could make the maximum profit. Thus the slaves were fed only enough to keep them well until a few days before the auction. Then various tricks were resorted to so that on the day of the auction the slaves would look healthy, although they

might in reality be quite ill. To the slave trader, it did not matter, as long as the new owner did not find out until after the sale.

When he go to sell a slave, he feed that one good for a few days, then when he goes to put 'em up on the auction block he takes a meat skin and greases all around that nigger's mouth and makes 'em look like they been eating plenty meat and such like and was good and strong and able to work. Sometimes he sell the babes from the breast, and then again he sell the mothers from the babes and the husbands and wives, and so on. He wouldn't let 'em holler much when the folks be sold away. He say, "I have you whupped if you don't hush." They [the slave trader and his wife] sure loved their six children, though. They wouldn't want nobody buying them.

JENNY PROCTOR
Botkin, p. 91.

An auction was synonymous with the breaking up of families. The most emotional scenes took place at the foot of the auction block.

My brothers and sisters were bid off first, and one by one, while my mother, paralyzed with grief, held me by the hand. Her turn came and she was bought by Issac Riley of Montgomery County. Then I was offered. . . . My mother, half distracted with the thought of parting forever from all her children, pushed through the crowd while the bid-

ding for me was going on, to the spot where Riley was
standing. She fell at his feet, and clung to his knees, en-
treating him in tones that a mother could only command,
to buy her baby as well as herself, and spare to her one,
at least, of her little ones. . . . This man disengag[ed] himself from her with . . . violent blows and kicks. . . . I must
have been then between five and six years old.

Henson, pp. 12–13.

*Occasionally a slave owner would try to be gentle
with a child. Before purchasing the child, a few would
attempt to make friends and persuade the child to come
with them. This kind of concern, however, never alle-
viated the child's pain of being separated from its
family.*

Major Ellison bought me and carried me to Mississippi. I
didn't want to go. They 'zamine you just like they do a
horse; they look at your teeth, and pull your eyelids back
and look at your eyes, and feel you just like you was a
horse. He 'zamined me and said, "Where's your mother?"
I said, "I don't know where my mother is, but I know
her." He said, "Would you know your mother if you saw
her?" I said, "Yes, sir. I would know her. I don't know
where she is, but I would know her." They had done sold
her then. He said, "Do you want us to buy you?" I said,
"No. I don't want you to buy me. I want to stay here."
He said, "We'll be nice to you and give you plenty to eat."
I said, "No, you won't have much to eat. What do you

have to eat?'' He said, "Lots of peas and cottonseed and things like that." But I said, "No, I'd rather stay here because I get plenty of pot licker and bread and buttermilk, and I don't want to go; I got plenty." I didn't know that that wasn't lots to eat. He said, "Well, I have married your mistress and she wants me to buy you." But I still said, "I don't want to go." They had done sold my mother to Mr. Armstrong then. So he kept talking to me, and he said, "Don't you want to see your sister?" I said, "Yes, but I don't want to go there to see her." They had sold her to Mississippi before that, and I knowed she was there, but I didn't want to go.

I went on back home, and the next day the old white woman whipped me, and I said to myself, "I wish that old white man had bought me." I didn't know he had bought me anyhow, but soon they took my cotton dresses and put 'em in a box, and they combed my hair, and I heard them tell me that Mr. Ellison had done come after me and he was in a buggy. I wanted to ride in the buggy, but I didn't want to go with him. So when I saw him I had a bucket of water on my head, and I set it on the shelf and ran just as fast as I could for the woods. They caught me, and Aunt Bet said, "Honey, don't do that. Mr. Ellison done bought you and you must go with him." She tied my clothes up in a bundle and he had me sitting up in the buggy with him, and we started to his house here. I had to get down to open the gate, and when I got back up I got behind in the little seat for servants, and he told me to come back and get inside, but I said I could ride behind up to the house, and he let me stay there, but he kept watching me. He was scared I would run away, because I had done run away that morning, but I wasn't going to run away, 'cause I wouldn't know which way to go after I got that far away.

ANONYMOUS
Fisk, pp. 191–192.

Even more rare was the occasion when the auction block became a source of joy.

I saw slaves sold. I can see that block now. My cousin Eliza was a pretty girl, really good-looking. Her master was her father. When the girls in the big house had beaus coming to see them, they'd ask, "Who is that pretty gal?" So they decided to get rid of her right away. The day they sold her will always be remembered. They stripped her to be bid off and looked at. I wasn't allowed to stand in the crowd. I was laying down under a big bush. The man that bought Eliza was from New York. The Negroes had made up 'nough money to buy her off themselves, but they wouldn't let that happen. There was a man bidding for her who was a big Swedelander. He always bid for the good-looking colored gals and bought 'em for his own use. He asked the man from New York, "What you gonna do with her when you get her?" The man from New York said, "None of your damn business, but you ain't got money enough to buy her." When the man from New York had

done bought her, he said, "Eliza, you are free from now
on."

DOC DANIEL DOWDY
Botkin, p. 155.

*A slave had no way of knowing what sort of treat-
ment he would receive at the hands of his new master.
However, when the sale took place in an area where
the slave had lived for many years, he had the advantage
of knowing the people who bid on him.*

When I was fifteen years old, I was brought to the court-
house, put up on the auction block to be sold. Old Judge
Miller was there. I knew him well because he was one of
the wealthiest slave owners in the county and the meanest
one. He was so cruel all the slaves and many owners hated
him because of it. He saw me on the block for sale and he
knew I was a good worker so when he bid for me I spoke
right out on the auction block and told him: "Judge Miller!
Don't you bid for me, 'cause if you do, I would not live
on your plantation. I will take a knife and cut my own
throat from ear to ear before I would be owned by you."

DELICIA PATTERSON
Library of Congress

*Once sold to a trader, the slaves were chained to-
gether and marched away, sleeping in the woods and
fields at night, until they reached their destination some
weeks later. Once there, the slave trader rested them for*

· 52 · TO BE A SLAVE

*a few days, gave them new clothing, and sold them to
new masters who would march them to the plantations.
These would be their "homes" until they were sold
again, escaped, or died.*

*The slave coffle was a familiar sight in many parts
of the South.*

The sun was shining out very hot, and in turning an angle
of the road we encountered the following group: First, a
little cart drawn by one horse, in which five or six half-
naked black children were tumbled like pigs together. The
cart had no covering, and they seemed to have been broiled
to sleep. Behind the cart marched three black women, with
head, neck and breasts uncovered, and without shoes or
stockings; next came three men, bareheaded, half naked,
and chained together with an ox-chain. Last of all came a
white man . . . on horseback, carrying pistols in his
belt.

Written by J. K. Spaulding, Secretary of the
Navy under President Martin van Buren.
The Negro in Virginia, p. 161.

*The slave coffles were usually seen on the dusty
southern roads between the months of October and
May, for it was during that time that the plantation
work was the lightest and a slave on a new plantation
had time to get adjusted before the hardest work season
began. However, the slave coffle itself was sometimes
such a torturous experience that many died on route*

and the survivors were hardly fit for anything but death by the time they reached the end.

My new master, whose name I did not hear, took me that same day across the Patuxent, where I joined fifty-one other slaves whom he had bought in Maryland. Thirty-two of these were men, and nineteen were women. The women were merely tied together with a rope, about the size of a bed cord, which was tied like a halter round the neck of each; but the men, of whom I was the stoutest and strongest, were very differently caparisoned. A strong iron collar was closely fitted by means of a padlock round each of our necks. A chain of iron about a hundred feet in length was passed through the hasp of each padlock, except at the two ends, where the hasps of the padlocks passed through a link of the chain. In addition to this, we were handcuffed in pairs, with iron staples and bolts, with a short chain about a foot long uniting the handcuffs and their wearers in pairs. In this manner, we were chained alternately by the right and left hand; and the poor man to whom I was thus ironed wept like an infant when the blacksmith with his heavy hammer fastened the ends of the bolts that kept the staples from slipping from our arms. For my own part, I felt indifferent to my fate. It appeared to me that the worst had come, and that no change of fortune could harm me.

Ball, p. 30.

I was born in Georgia, in Norcross, and I'm ninety years

old. My father's name was Roger Stielszen and my mother's name was Betty. Massa Early Stielszen captures them in Africa and brung them to Georgia. He got killed and my sister and me went to his son. His son was a killer. He got in trouble in Georgia and got him two good-stepping horses and the covered wagon. Then he chains all his slaves round the necks and fastens the chains to the hosses and makes them walk all the way to Texas. My mother and my sister had to walk. Emma was my sister. Somewhere on the road it went to snowing, and massa wouldn't let us wrap anything round her feet. We had to sleep on the ground, too, in all that snow.

Massa have a great, long whip platted out of rawhide, and when one of the slaves fall behind or give out, he hit him with that whip. It take the hide every time he hit a slave. Mother, she give out on the way, 'bout the line of Texas. Her feet got raw and bleeding, and her legs swoll plumb out of shape. Then massa, he just take out his gun and shot her, and while she lay dying, he kicks her two, three times, and say, "Damn a nigger what can't stand nothing." You know that man, he wouldn't bury Mother. Just leave her laying where he shot her at.

BEN SIMPSON
Botkin, p. 75.

Sometimes the slaves were kept overnight and longer at a specially built slave jail, while the slave trader went around to the neighboring plantations to buy more slaves. He would then add these to his coffle, and pistol

*on his hip, march them down the road, and sometimes
to the railroad for the long journey to the deep South.*

They would come in on foot . . . each one carrying an old
tow sack on his back with everything he's got in it. Over
the hills they would come in lines reaching as far as you
could see. They walked in double lines chained together in
twos. The slavers walked them here to the railroad and
shipped them in coal cars to the cotton country.

LORENZO IVY
The Negro in Virginia, p. 172.

Had a slave jail built at the crossroads with iron bars 'cross
the windows. Soon as the coffle get there, they bring all
the slaves from the jail two at a time and string 'em along
the chain back of the other po' slaves. Everybody in the
villages come out—especially the wives and sweethearts and
mothers—to see their sold-off children for the last time.
And when they start the chain a-clanking and step off down
the line, they all just sing and shout and make all the noises
they can, trying to hide the sorrow in their hearts and cover
up the cries and moaning of them they were leaving behind.
Oh, Lord!

SIS SHACKELFORD
The Negro in Virginia, p. 173.

*Not all slaves marched in coffles. Some were shipped
by steamboat. Solomon Northup was one of these. He
was one of the many blacks who was born free in the*

*North, kidnapped by slave traders, and sold into slavery.
For twelve years he worked as a slave in Louisiana
before regaining his freedom.*

We left the steamboat *Rodolph* at a place called Alexandria,
several hundred miles from New Orleans. It is a small
town on the southern shore of Red River. Having remained
there overnight, we entered the morning train of cars and
were soon at Bayou Lamourie, a still smaller place, distance
eighteen miles from Alexandria. At that time it was the
termination of the railroad. Ford's plantation was situated
on the Texas road, twelve miles from Lamourie, in the
Great Pine Woods. This distance it was announced to us,
must be traveled on foot. Accordingly we all set out in
the company of Ford. It was an excessively hot day. . . .
The whole country about Red River is low and marshy. The
Pine Woods, as they are called, is comparatively upland
with frequent small intervals, however, running through
them. This upland is covered with numerous trees—the
white oak, the chincopin, resembling chestnut, but principally the yellow pine. They are of great size, running up
sixty feet, and perfectly straight. The woods were full of
cattle, very shy and wild, dashing away in herds, with a
loud snuff, at our approach. Some of them were marked
or branded, the rest appeared to be in their wild and un-
tamed state. They are much smaller than northern breeds,
and the peculiarity about them that most attracted my attention was their horns. They stand out from the sides of the
head precisely sraight, like two iron spikes.

At noon we reached a cleared piece of ground containing three or four acres. . . . After a long rest we set forth again, following the Texas road, which had the appearance of being very rarely traveled. For five miles we passed through continuous woods without observing a single habitation. At length, just as the sun was sinking in the west, we entered another opening, containing some twelve or fifteen acres.

In this opening stood a house. . . . It was two stories high, with a piazza in front. In the rear of it was also a log kitchen, poultry house, corncribs, and several negro cabins. Near the house was a peach orchard, and gardens of orange and pomegranate trees. The space was entirely surrounded by woods, and covered with a carpet of rich, rank verdure. It was a quiet, lonely, pleasant place—literally a green spot in the wilderness. It was the residence of my master, William Ford.

Northup, pp. 92–122.

It was also to be the residence of Solomon Northup, slave. This was the plantation, a world within itself, the stage upon which the slaves acted out the parts assigned to them and, at the same time, lived their lives.

THE PLANTATION

· 1 ·

The plantation. It was a large white mansion, with fluted columns and a broad porch; massive trees spread their limbs over a circular driveway which led up to the house. From the carriages which rolled up the driveway stepped finely dressed men and women, the aristocracy of southern culture. Once inside the mansion, these ladies and gentlemen sat beneath chandeliers in high-ceilinged rooms and discoursed on the topics of the day. And all the while they were attended to by unobtrusive, attentive, and faithful Negro slaves. Somewhere, in the background, out of sight, were the slave quarters with their inhabitants.

Such is the picture that is often presented of the southern plantation. It is not a true one. There were a few plantations which fit the above description, but these were the exceptions. Most plantation owners lived modestly and some even poorly.

In the slave-holding South, the more slaves a man owned, the more respected he was. In other words, the more human beings he held by force and against their will, the more highly regarded he was. It is generally thought that all slave owners held hundreds of slaves. The reality was quite different. In 1860 there were 384,884 slave owners in the South. Of that number, less than three thousand owned more than one hundred slaves. The overwhelming majority of slaveholders held less than twenty slaves. Yet, even if a man only held one or two slaves, he had considerably more status in southern society than a man who held no slaves. As a group, the slave owners controlled the South, even though they were a decided minority. Fully three fourths of the South's white population held no slaves. But the economy of the South was built upon slavery, even though that slavery profited only one fourth of the white population and the black population not at all.

· 2 ·

The plantation was a world in itself. It was composed of the slave owner's house, the "big house," as the slaves called it. There was "slave row," the line of little cabins which the slaves called "home" for lack of a better term. Situated near "slave row" was the house of the overseer. Scattered about the plantation were various barns and sheds where animals, tools, and the harvested crops were stored. And surrounding every-

thing were fields and woods, beyond which, somewhere, was freedom.

My master's house was of brick (brick houses are by no means common amongst the planters, whose residences are generally built of frame work, weather-boarded with pine boards, and covered with shingles of the white cedar or juniper cypress), and contained two large parlors and a spacious hall or entry on the ground floor. The main building was two stories high; and attached to this was a smaller building, one story and a half high, with a large room, where the family generally took breakfast; with a kitchen at the farther extremity from the main building.

There was a spacious garden behind the house, containing I believe, about five acres, well cultivated and handsomely laid out. . . . At one end of the main building was a small house, called the library, in which my master kept his books and papers, and where he spent much of his time.

At some distance from the mansion was a pigeon house, and near the kitchen was a large wooden building, called the kitchen quarter, in which the house servants slept, and where they generally took their meals. Here, also, the washing of the family was done, and all the rough or unpleasant work of the kitchen department, such as cleaning and scaling fish, putting up pork, etc., was assigned to this place.

There was no barn on this plantation . . . but there was a wooden building about forty feet long, called the coach house, in one end of which the family carriage and the chaise in which my master rode were kept. Under the same roof was a stable, sufficiently capacious to contain ten or twelve horses. In one end of the building the corn intended for the horses was kept, and the whole of the loft or upper story was occupied by the fodder or blades and tops of the corn.

Ball, pp. 119–122.

The houses of the slaves were generally more fit for animals than human beings. There were a few notable exceptions, however. One of these was the houses Thomas Jefferson built for his slaves at Monticello, which were "the envy of all Albemarle County" and better than the houses of average white men.

Their quarters were comfortable brick dwellings with real floors, doors that shut tight, and windows with glass panes. . . . Jefferson's "slave row" at Monticello was a continuous brick structure, built into the side of the hill, and partitioned into one-room cabins. . . .

The Negro in Virginia, pp. 38, 67.

More typical were the houses George Washington built for his slaves. Julian Niemcewicz, a Polish poet, spent two weeks at Mout Vernon in 1798 and wrote this description of conditions there.

We entered some negroes' huts, for their habitations cannot be called houses. They are far more miserable than the poorest of the cottages of our peasants. The husband and his wife sleep on a miserable bed, the children on the floor. A very poor chimney, a little kitchen furniture stands amid this misery—a teakettle and cups. A boy about fifteen was lying on the floor with an attack of dreadful convulsions. The general had sent to Alexandria for a physician. A small orchard with vegetables was situated close to the hut. Five or six hens, each with ten or fifteen chickens, walked there. That is the only pleasure allowed to negroes. They are not permitted to keep either ducks or geese or pigs. They sell the chickens in Alexandria and buy with the money some furniture. They receive a peck of Indian corn every week, and half of it is for the children, besides twenty herrings in a month. They receive a cotton jacket and a pair of breeches yearly. The general possesses 300 negroes, excepting women and children of which a part belongs to Mrs. Washington. . . .

The Negro in Virginia, pp. 67–68.

And from the slaves' point of view the picture was even more grim.

The softest couches in the world are not to be found in the log mansion of the slaves. The one whereon I reclined year after year was a plank twelve inches wide and ten feet long. My pillow was a stick of wood. The bedding was a coarse blanket and not a rag or shred beside. Moss might be used, were it not that it directly breeds a swarm of fleas. The cabin is constructed of logs, without floor or window.

The latter is altogether unnecessary, the crevices between the logs admitting sufficient light. In stormy weather the rain drives through them, rendering it comfortless and extremely disagreeable. The rude door hangs on wooden hinges. In one end is constructed an awkward fireplace.

Northup, pp. 170–171.

We lodged in log huts and on the bare ground. Wooden floors were an unknown luxury. In a single room were huddled, like cattle, ten or a dozen persons, men, women and children. All ideas of refinement and decency were, of course, out of the question. There were neither bedsteads, nor furniture of any description. Our beds were collections of straw and old rags, thrown down in the corners and boxed in with boards, a single blanket the only covering. Our favorite way of sleeping, however, was on a plank, our heads raised on an old jacket and our feet toasting before the smouldering fire. The wind whistled and the rain and snow blew in through the cracks, and the damp earth soaked in the moisture till the floor was miry as a pigsty. Such were our houses.

The principal food of those upon my master's plantation consisted of cornmeal and salt herrings, to which was added in summer a little buttermilk and the few vegetables which each might raise for himself and his family on the little piece of ground which was assigned to him for the purpose, called a truck patch.

In ordinary times we had two regular meals in a day: breakfast at twelve o'clock, after laboring from daylight, and supper when the work of the remainder of the day was over. In harvest season we had three. Our dress was of tow cloth; for the children nothing but a shirt; for the older ones a pair of pantaloons or a gown in addition, according to the sex. Besides these, in the winter a round jacket or overcoat, a wool hat once in two or three years, for the males, and a pair of coarse shoes once a year.

Henson, pp. 17–18.

· 3 ·

The plantation. It was like a country unto itself, and within its confines, large or small, life was generally the same for the slave.

His principal occupation was work, and the work with which he was principally occupied was cotton. It was a crop that needed much care and long hours of tedious work. One could tell the month of the year by what work was being done on the cotton. Some crops can be planted, hoed, and left to grow until time for harvest. Not cotton.

The ground is prepared by throwing up beds, or ridges, with the plough—back-furrowing, it is called. Oxen and mules, the latter almost exclusively, are used in ploughing. The women as frequently as the men perform this labor, feeding, currying, and taking care of their teams and in all respects doing the field and stable work. . . .

The beds, or ridges, are six feet wide, that is from water furrow to water furrow. A plough drawn by one mule is then run along the top of the ridge or center of the bed, making the drill, into which a girl usually drops the seed, which she carries in a bag hung round her neck. Behind her comes a mule and harrow, covering up the seed, so that two mules, three slaves, a plough and harrow are employed in planting a row of cotton. This is done in the months of March and April. . . .

When there are no cold rains, the cotton usually makes its appearance in a week. In the course of eight or ten days afterwards the first hoeing is commenced. This is performed in part, also, by the aid of the plough and mule. The plough passes as near as possible to the cotton on both sides, throwing the furrow from it. Slaves follow with their hoes, cutting up the grass and cotton, leaving hills two feet and a half apart. This is called scraping cotton. In two weeks more, commences the second hoeing. This time the furrow is thrown towards the cotton. Only one stalk, the largest is now left standing in each hill. In another fortnight it is hoed the third time, throwing the furrow towards the cotton in the same manner as before and killing all the grass between the rows. About the first of July, when it is a foot high or thereabouts, it is hoed the fourth and last time. Now the whole space between the rows is ploughed, leaving a deep water furrow in the center. During all these hoeings . . . the fastest hoer takes the lead row. He is usually about a rod in advance of his companions. If one of them passes him, he is whipped. If one falls behind or is

a moment idle, he is whipped. In fact, the lash is flying from morning until night, the whole day long. The hoeing season thus continues from April until July, a field having no sooner been finished once than it is commenced again.

Northup, pp. 163–165.

In the latter part of August, the cottonpicking season begins.

. . . each slave is presented with a sack. A strap is fastened to it, which goes over the neck, holding the mouth of the sack breast high, while the bottom nearly reaches to the ground. Each one is also presented with a large basket that will hold about two barrels. This is to put the cotton in when the sack is filled. The baskets are carried to the field and placed at the beginning of the rows.

The cotton grows from five to seven feet high, each stalk having a great many branches shooting out in all directions and lapping each other above the water furrow.

There are few sights more pleasant to the eye than a wide cotton field when it is in the bloom. It presents an appearance of purity, like an immaculate expanse of light, new-fallen snow.

Sometimes the slave picks down one side of a row and back upon the other, but more usually there is one on either side, gathering all that has blossomed, leaving the unopened bolls for a succeeding picking. When the sack is filled, it is emptied into the basket and trodden down. It is necessary to be extremely careful the first time going through the field, in order not to break the branches off the stalks. The cotton will not bloom upon a broken branch. . . . I had had no experience whatever in cotton picking. It was an awkward business indeed. While others used both hands, snatching the cotton and depositing it in the mouth of the sack with a precision and dexterity that was incomprehensible to me, I had to seize the boll with one hand and deliberately draw out the white, gushing blossom with the other. Depositing the cotton in the sack, moreover, was a difficulty that demanded the exercise of both hands and eyes. I was compelled to pick it from the ground where it would fall nearly as often as from the stalk where it had grown. I made havoc also with the branches loaded with the yet unbroken bolls, the long, cumbersome sack swinging from side to side in a manner not allowable in the cotton field.

Northup, pp. 166–167, 178.

From the time the stars began to fade from the sky in the morning until they reappeared in the evening, the slaves worked at cotton and at everything else which had to be done on the plantation. Each day ended as the previous one had. Each one began as the previous one had. And each day expended itself as the previous one had.

Yes, sir, I can hear it now. Ol' overseer used to blow us out at sunrise on the conker shell—"Toot—toot!" Had to get your breakfast before day, 'cause you got to be in the field when the sun gets to showing itself about the trees.

WEST TURNER
The Negro in Virginia, p. 60.

I think about one hundred and sixty-eight assembled this morning at the sound of the horn—two or three being sick sent word to the overseer that they could not come. . . . The overseer then led off to the field with his horn in one hand and his whip in the other, we following—men, women and children, promiscuously—and a wretched looking troop we were. There was not an entire garment among us.

More than half of the gang was entirely naked. Several young girls who had arrived at puberty, wearing only the livery with which nature had ornamented them, and a great number of lads of an equal or superior age, appeared in the same custom. There was neither bonnet, cap, nor headdress of any kind amongst us, except the old straw hat that I wore. . . . Some of the men had old shirts and some ragged trousers, but no one wore both. Amongst the women several wore petticoats and many had shifts. Not one of the whole number wore both of these vestments.

We walked nearly a mile through one vast cotton field before we arrived at the place of our intended day's labor.

Ball, pp. 128–129.

An hour before daylight the horn is blown. Then the slaves arouse, prepare their breakfast, fill a gourd with water, in another, deposit their dinner of cold bacon and corn cake, and hurry to the field again. It is an offense invariably followed by a flogging to be found at the quarters after daybreak. Then the fears and labors of another day begin and until its close there is no such thing as rest.

. . . with the exception of ten or fifteen minutes, which is given them at noon to swallow their allowance of cold bacon, they are not permitted to be a moment idle until it is too dark to see, and when the moon is full, they oftentimes labor till the middle of the night. They do not dare to stop even at dinner time, nor return to the quarters, however late it be, until the order to halt is given by the driver.

Northup, pp. 167, 170.

When the order to halt was finally given, it was weighing-in time. Each slave was expected to pick at least two hundred pounds of cotton a day. That was the minimum for everybody. Generally the overseer learned how much more than that each slave could pick, and that was his daily task.

The day's work over in the field, the baskets are "toted," or in other words, carried to the ginhouse where the cotton is weighed. No matter how fatigued and weary he may be —no matter how much he longs for sleep and rest—a slave never approaches the ginhouse with his basket of cotton but with fear. If it falls short in weight—if he has not performed the full task appointed him—he knows that he must suffer. And if he has exceeded it by ten or twenty pounds, in all probability his master will measure the next day's task accordingly. . . .

It was rarely that a day passed by without one or more whippings. This occurred at the time the cotton was weighed. The delinquent, whose weight had fallen short, was taken out, stripped, made to lie upon the ground, face downwards, when he received a punishment proportioned to his offense. It is the literal, unvarnished truth that the crack of the lash and the shrieking of the slaves can be heard from dark till bedtime on Epps' plantation, any day almost during the entire period of the cotton-picking season.

The number of lashes is graduated according to the nature of the case. Twenty-five are deemed a mere brush, inflicted, for instance, when a dry leaf or a piece of boll is found in the cotton, or when a branch is broken in the field. Fifty is ordinary penalty following all delinquencies of the next higher grade. One hundred is called severe; it is the punishment inflicted for the serious offense of standing idle in the field.

Northup, pp. 175–177, 179–180.

Every night after work was over, us slaves had to gin cotton. Course they had the gin machine, but it never worked fast as us niggers would pick the cotton and was always breaking down.

See that foot? Wears a size fourteen shoe, I does, and near as I can recollect, it was the same size in them days. Well, sir, everybody had to gin a shoe full of cotton at night before going to bed. Ol' overseer would make the old women pack everybody's shoe tight with cotton and they got to see that shoe full. I had such a big pile that the others used to finish a long time before me. They all used to laugh at me and joke while they was ginnin', 'cause I got such a lot to do. I used to wrap my feet up in rags nights so as to keep 'em from gettin' any bigger, but it didn't help any.

WEST TURNER
The Negro in Virginia, pp. 64–65.

Yet once the slaves left the field, their work was far from finished.

Each one must then attend to his respective chores. One feeds the mules, another the swine—another cuts the wood, and so forth. Finally, at a late hour, they reach the quarters, sleepy and overcome with the long day's toil. Then a fire must be kindled in the cabin, the corn ground in the small hand-mill, and supper and dinner for the next day in the field prepared. All that is allowed them is corn and bacon, which is given out at the corncrib and smokehouse every Sunday morning. Each one receives, as his weekly allowance, three and a half pounds of bacon, and corn enough to make a peck of meal. That is all—no tea, coffee, sugar, and with the exception of a very scanty sprinkling now and then, no salt. . . .

When the corn is ground and fire is made, the bacon is taken down from the nail on which it hangs, a slice cut off and thrown upon the coals to broil. The majority of slaves have no knife, much less a fork. They cut their bacon with the axe at the woodpile. The corn meal is mixed with a little water, placed in the fire, and baked. When it is "done brown," the ashes are scraped off, and being placed upon a chip which answers for a table, the tenant of the slave hut is ready to sit down upon the ground to supper.

By this time it is usually midnight. The same fear of punishment with which they approach the ginhouse, possesses them again on lying down to get a snatch of rest. It is the fear of oversleeping in the morning. Such an offense would certainly be attended with not less than twenty lashes. With a prayer that he may be on his feet and wide awake at the first sound of the horn, he sinks to his slumbers nightly.

Northup, pp. 168–170.

To the sound of the whip and the shrieks of black men and women, the slave owner and America grew wealthy. Yet it is all the more remarkable that even now the two hundred years of slavery are looked upon matter-of-factly and not as a time of unrelieved horror.

While there were many whites who recognized and fought against the inhumanity of slavery, the majority were much like the northerner who visited a southern plantation and described being awakened by the overseer's horn.

I soon hear the tramp of the laborers passing along the avenue. . . . All is soon again still as midnight. . . . I believe that I am the only one in the house that the bell disturbs; yet I do not begrudge the few minutes loss of sleep it causes me, it sounds so pleasantly in the half dreamy morning.

ANONYMOUS
Stampp, p. 44.

Perhaps the sound of other human beings marching to the fields for another day of forced labor was a "pleasant" one. Perhaps. But to those who made the sound, it was the dull monotonous sound of the living deaths in which they were held captive.

4

RESISTANCE TO
SLAVERY—1

· 1 ·

There are two ways in which a man can be enslaved.

*One is through force. He can be penned behind
fences, guarded constantly, punished severely for breaking the slightest rule, and made to live in constant fear.*

*The second is to teach him to think that his own
best interests will be served by doing what his master
wishes him to do. He can be taught that he is inferior
and that only through slavery will he eventually rise
to the "level" of his master.*

The southern slave owner used both.

*The first was the way of the whip, the threat of the
auction block, and murder. Its aim was to make the
slave live in constant fear, the kind of fear that
Solomon Northup described so vividly in the previous
chapter.*

*The second way was more subtle. Its aim was to
brainwash the slave, to destroy his mind and replace*

*it with the mind of the master. In that way the slave
would enslave himself and there would be no need to
police him. A slave should have no sense of himself
that was separate from the self the master wanted him
to have. Thus it was that no black had a name of his
own. He was given the surname of his owner, no matter
how many owners he might have during his life.*

A Negro has got no name. My father was a Ransom and
he had a uncle named Hankin. If you belong to Mr. Jones
and he sell you to Mr. Johnson, consequently you go by the
name of your owner. Now where you get a name? We are
wearing the name of our master. I was first a Hale; then
my father was sold and then I was named Reed.

ANONYMOUS
Bontemps-Hughes, p. 56.

*Without a name of his own, the slave's ability to see
himself apart from his owner was lessened. He was
never asked who he was. He was asked, "Who's nigger
are you?" The slave had no separate identity. He was
always Mr. So-and-so's nigger.*

*Another instrument used to control the minds of the
slaves was religion. No slave owner allowed his slaves
to attend church by themselves, fearing that they would
use the opportunity to plan an insurrection rather than
thank God that they had such "good" masters. So, the
slave owner either did the preaching himself or hired
a white preacher, or let a trusted slave preach. The only*

preaching a slave owner approved of was that which would make the slave happy to be a slave.

This the way it go: Be nice to massa and missus; don't be mean; be obedient, and work hard. That was all the Sunday school lesson they taught us.

WEST TURNER
The Negro in Virginia, p. 108.

. . . in Missouri, and as far as I have any knowledge of slavery in the other states, the religious teaching consists of teaching the slave that he must never strike a white man; that God made him for a slave; and that, when whipped, he must not find fault—for the Bible says, "He that knoweth his master's will and doeth it not, shall be beaten with many stripes!" And slaveholders find such religion very profitable to them.

Brown, p. 82.

"Poor creatures! you little consider, when you are idle and neglectful of your masters' business, when you steal, and waste, and hurt any of their substance, when you are saucy and impudent, when you are telling them lies and deceiving them, or when you prove stubborn and sullen, and will not do the work you are set about without stripes and vexation,—you do not consider, I say, that what faults you are guilty of towards your masters and mistresses are faults done against God Himself, who hath set your masters and mistresses over you in his own stead, and expects that you would do for them just as you would do for Him. . . . your masters and mistresses are God's overseers, and that, if you are faulty towards them, God Himself will punish you severely for it in the next world, unless you repent of it, and strive to make amends by your faithfulness and diligence for the time to come.

Sermon of a white preacher to Virginia slaves
Olmstead, p. 119.

Few slaves found arguments of this kind very convincing. However, from this religion which was preached to them they took what they needed and could use. They fashioned their own kind of Christianity, which they turned to for strength in the constant times of need. In the Old Testament story of the enslavement of the Hebrews by the Egyptians, they found their own story. In the figure of Jesus Christ, they found someone who had suffered as they suffered, someone who understood, someone who offered them rest from their suffering. They so transformed the religion of the slave owner that eventually they came to look down upon the white preachers and white religious services.

That ol' white preachin' wasn't nothin'. . . . Ol' white preacher used to talk with their tongues without saying nothin', but Jesus told us slaves to talk with our hearts.

NANCY WILLIAMS
The Negro in Virginia, p. 108.

There was an old man who would answer the preacher every Sunday meetin'. He made so much noise ol' massa said, "John, if you stop makin' that noise in church, I'll give you a new pair of boots." John said, "I'll try, Massa." The next meetin' he tried and tried to be quiet so he could get his new boots, but the spirit got him and he yelled out, "Glory to God! Boots or no boots, glory to God!"

JULIA FRASIER
The Negro in Virginia, p. 108.

Religion also presented the slaves with the idea that they would receive their reward after they died. This appealed to their minds, but they weren't necessarily convinced that the way to the promised heaven was through obedience to their owners. And sometimes they questioned the nature of that life after death and the heaven it promised.

Uncle Silas was near 'bout a hundred, I reckon—too feeble to do no work, but always got strength enough to hobble to church when the slave service gonna be. Ol' preacher was Reverend Johnson—forget the rest of his name. He was a-preachin' and the slaves was sittin' there sleepin' and fannin' theyselves with oak branches, and Uncle Silas got up in the front row of the slave's pew and halted Reverend Johnson. "Is us slaves gonna be free in Heaven?" Uncle Silas asked. The preacher stopped and looked at Uncle Silas like he wanta kill him, 'cause no one ain't supposed to say nothing except "Amen" while he was preaching. Waited a minute he did, lookin' hard at Uncle Silas standin' there, but didn't give no answer. "Is God gonna free us slaves

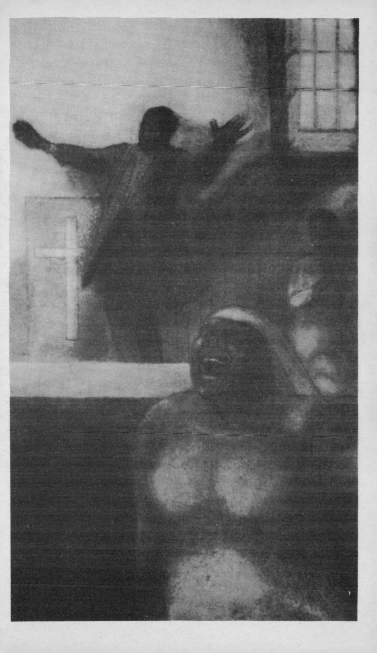

when we get to Heaven?" Uncle Silas yelled. Ol' white preacher pulled his handkerchief and wiped the sweat from his face. "Jesus says come unto Me ye who are free from sin and I will give you salvation." "Gonna give us freedom 'long with salvation?" ask Uncle Silas. "The Lord gives and the Lord takes away, and he that is without sin is going to have life everlasting." Then he went ahead preachin', fast-like, without paying no attention to Uncle Silas. But Uncle Silas wouldn't sit down; stood there the rest of the service, he did, and that was the last time he come to church. Uncle Silas died before another preachin' time come around. Guess he found out whether he gonna be free sooner than he calculated to.

BEVERLY JONES
The Negro in Virginia, p. 109.

The slave thought of heaven, but just as he made the white man's religion his own, he had his own heaven.

The slaves who are natives of this country . . . believe that those who have tormented them here will most surely be tormented in their turn hereafter. . . . They are ready enough to receive the faith which conducts them to heaven and eternal rest on account of their present sufferings; but they by no means so willingly admit the master and mistress to an equal participation in their enjoyments. . . . According to their notions, the master and mistress are to be, in future, the companion of wicked slaves, whilst an agreeable recreation of the celestial inhabitants of the negro's heaven will be a return to the overseer of the countless lashes that he has lent out so liberally here.

It is impossible to reconcile the mind of the native slave to the idea of living in a state of perfect equality and boundless affection with the white people. Heaven will be no heaven to him if he is not to be avenged of his enemies. I know from experience that these are the fundamental rules of his religious creed, because I learned them in the religious meetings of the slaves themselves.

Ball, pp. 189–190.

The slave had many means of resisting the dehumanizing effects of slavery. Religion became one of them. It became a purifying force in the life of the slaves, a release from the everyday misery. And through the religious songs they made up from Biblical stories, they expressed their real feelings about slavery.

Didn't my Lord deliver Daniel,
Deliver Daniel, deliver Daniel?
Didn't my Lord deliver Daniel,
Then why not every man?

He delivered Daniel from the lion's den,
Jonah from the belly of the whale,
The Hebrew children from the fiery furnace,
Then why not every man?

Joshua fit the battle of Jericho,
Jericho, Jericho.

Joshua fit the battle of Jericho,
And the walls come tumbling down.

Oh Mary, don't you weep, don't you moan
Oh Mary, don't you weep, don't you moan
'Cause Pharaoh's army got drownded,
Oh Mary, don't you weep.

One of these mornings at five o'clock
This ol' world's gonna reel and rock.
Pharoah's army got drownded,
Oh Mary, don't you weep.

Don't know what my mother wants to stay here for.
This ol' world ain't no friend to her., etc.

And in one of the greatest black religious songs, the slaves took the story of Samson, and with their genius for going to the core of an experience, they put these words into Samson's mouth and expressed their deepest feelings.

If I had my way,
If I had my way,
If I had my way,
I'd tear this building down.

· 2 ·

In the slave owner's attempts to control the minds of the slaves, one of the most constant ideas was the natural superiority of the white man and the natural inferiority of the black. The slave owner profaned the Portuguese word for black, "Negro," and made it "nigger." It was a brutal, violent word that stung the soul of the slave more than the whip did his back. But the slaves took this ugly word and, like the white man's religion, made it their own. In their mouths it became an affectionate, endearing word. As much as was possible they robbed it of its ability to spiritually maim them.

Not only, however, did they have to combat being defined by a curse word. Because of their dark skin color, thin curly hair, thick lips, and broad noses, they were regarded as oddities, as "creatures" who could be ridiculed. Even the way they talked was regarded as a sign of their inferiority. The slaves were in the process of trying to fashion the English language to their tongues. The African languages are musical, and one word can have many meanings depending on the intonation it is given. Thus it was difficult for them to be satisfied with the rather flat intonations of English, and they made their own kind of English, one that was more musical, more pleasant to the ear.

Perhaps the most eloquent discussion of black "inferiority" and white "superiority" was written by Thomas Jefferson, also the author of America's rhetoric of liberty.

The first difference which strikes us is that of color. Whether the black of the negro resides in the reticular membrane between the skin and scarf-skin, or in the scarf-skin itself; whether it proceeds from the color of the blood, the color of the bile, or from that of some other secretion, the difference is fixed in nature, and is as real as if its seat and cause were better known to us. And is this difference of no importance? Is it not the foundation of a greater or less share of beauty in the two races? Are not the fine mixtures of red and white, the expressions of every passion by greater or less suffusions of color in the one, preferable to that eternal monotony which reigns in the countenances, that immovable veil of black which covers all the emotions of the other race? . . . there are other physical distinctions proving a difference of race. They have less hair on the face and body. They secrete less by the kidneys, and more by the glands of the skin, which gives them a very strong and disagreeable odor. . . . They seem to require less sleep. A black after hard labor through the day, will be induced by the slightest amusements to sit up till midnight, or later, though knowing he must be out with the first dawn of the morning. They are at least as brave, and more adventuresome. But this may perhaps proceed from a want of forethought, which prevents their seeing a danger till it be present. . . . They are more ardent after their female; but love seems with them to be more an eager desire, than a tender delicate mixture of sentiment and sensation. Their griefs are transient. . . . In general, their existence appears to participate more of sensation than reflection. . . . Comparing them by their faculties of memory, reason, and imagination, it appears to me that in memory they are equal to the whites; in reason much inferior, as I think one could scarcely be found capable of tracing and comprehending the investigations of Euclid! and that in imagination they are dull, tasteless, and anomalous. . . . never yet could I find that a black had uttered a thought above the level of plain narration; never saw even an elementary trait of painting or sculpture. In music they are more generally gifted than the whites with accurate ears for tune and time, and they have been found capable of imagining a small catch. Whether they will be equal to the composition of a more extensive run of melody, or of complicated harmony, is yet to be proved. . . . I advance it therefore as a suspicion only, that the blacks . . . are inferior to the whites in the endowments of both body and mind.

"Notes on the State of Virginia"
Wish, pp. 225–226, 230.

Blacks who were born in this country had little with which to combat such ideas. They were born into slavery, lived in slavery, and died in slavery. What could they point to as proof that they were not inferior? Nothing, except a feeling within that it wasn't true.

Those slaves who were native Africans were more fortunate, in that they had former lives. Early in the nineteenth century, there were still many native Africans on plantations. Charles Ball was one American-born black who grew up listening to stories of Africa from

his grandfather and other Africans. They knew some-
thing else besides slavery.

The native Africans are revengeful, and unforgiving in
their tempers, easily provoked, and cruel in their designs.
They generally place little, or even no value upon the
fine houses and superb furniture of their masters; and
discover no beauty in the fair complexions, and delicate
form of their mistresses. They feel indignant at the
servitude that is imposed upon them and only want power
to inflict the most cruel retribution upon their oppressors;
but they desire only the means of subsistence and
temporary gratification in this country during their abode
here.

They are universally of the opinion, and this opinion is
founded in their religion, that after death they shall return
to their own country and rejoin their former companions
and friends in some happy region, in which they will be
provided with plenty of food and beautiful women from
the lovely daughters of their native land.

Ball, pp. 188–189.

*The slave who was born in America, however, had
"borrowed all his ideas, of present and future happiness,
from the opinions and intercourse of white people, and
of Christians," as Charles Ball pointed out. And some
accepted these ideas totally.*

. . . I thought as long as I stayed where the white folks

was, they would protect me from all harm, even the stars in the elements, storms, or whatnot. Just stay near the white folks and I had nothing to worry about. I thought white folks made the stars, sun and everything on the earth. I knowed nothing but to be driven and beat all the time. I seen 'em take the bottom rail out of the rail fences and stick the nigger's head in the hole, then jam the balance of the fence down on his neck and beat him till he's stiff.

EDWARD TAYLOR
Library of Congress

The slaves who most exemplified those qualities of obedience, submissiveness, and dependence have come to be known as Uncle Toms, the name being taken from the central character of Harriet Beecher Stowe's anti-slavery novel, Uncle Tom's Cabin. *(Mrs. Stowe got her idea for the character of Uncle Tom from Josiah Henson's autobiography.) Generally, these Uncle Toms were those slaves who had the most contact with the master and his family—the house servants. Because of this constant contact, the house servants were much more likely to be the model slaves that slaveholders dreamed of. Quite often a house servant was trained to his duty from childhood. He was separated from the other slaves, and from that time on, he slept on a pallet on the floor of the owner's bedroom or outside his door. He was raised to believe that to be a house servant was the greatest honor that could come to him.*

My master gave me better clothes than the little slaves of my age generally received. . . . He often told me that he intended to make me his waiter, and that if I behaved well I should become his overseer in time. These stations of waiter and overseer appeared to me the highest points of honor and greatness in the whole world, and had not circumstances frustrated my master's plans, as well as my own views, I should probably have been living at this time in a cabin on the corner of some tobacco plantation.

Ball, p. 19.

On many plantations house servants were hated by the slaves who worked in the fields. These servants often took their masters' interests so seriously that they acted as spies for them. House servants were responsible for uncovering and revealing to slave owners innumerable planned slave insurrections.

They taught us to be against one another and no matter where you would go you would always find one that would tattle and have the white folks pecking on you. They would be trying to make it soft for themselves.

ANONYMOUS
Bontemps-Hughes, p. 47.

Many of them are the most despicable tale-bearers and mischief-makers, who will, for the sake of the favor of his master or mistress, frequently betray his fellow slave, and by tattling get him severely whipped; and for these acts . . . he is often rewarded by his master, who knows it is for his interest to keep such ones about him; though he is sometimes obliged, in addition to a reward, to send him away, for fear of the vengeance of the betrayed slaves.

AUSTIN STEWARD
Nichols, p. 75.

Sleeping in a room adjacent to the slaves, who were ironed, I discerned enough from their conversation to enable me to know that a mutiny was abroad, and that it was that intention of the slaves, in order to effect their freedom, to put to death all the whites on board, and that I, too, was included—owing to the attention that was paid me—with the doomed. By jests and cheerfulness with them, however, I gathered their detached hints from their every movement. That they had even then provided themselves with a file from the lot of blacksmith tools on board, and that many were at that moment free from their chains. This information I carried to my master; and after ascertaining the truth of my statement, he had them again bound more firmly than ever.

WILLIAM HAYDEN
Nichols, p. 85.

Charles Ball tried on two occasions to win his master's favor, though he was a field hand. In the first instance, he was instrumental in the capture of two slaves who had murdered the daughter of a neighboring slave owner. He received nothing for his effort, though. He tried to win his owner's favor again by building a fish trap on his own time and catching a number of fish.

I gave a large fish to the overseer and took three more to the great house. These were the first fresh fish that had been in the family this season and I was much praised by my master and young mistresses for my skill and success in fishing. But this was all the advantage I received from this effort to court the favor of the great. . . . The part I had performed in the detection of the murderers of the young lady was forgotten, or at least, not mentioned now. I went away from the house not only disappointed, but chagrined, and thought to myself that if my master and young mistresses had nothing but words to give me for my fish, we should not carry on a very large traffic.

Ball, pp. 238–239.

He was only interested in the welfare of his owner to the degree that his own needs and interests were served. This was the typical attitude of the field hand.

Many house slaves, however, shared the attitudes of the field hand. They used their positions inside the "great house" to spy on the master, not for him.

Was serving gal for missus. Used to have to stand behind her at the table and reach her the salt and syrup and anything else she called for. Ol' massa would spell out real fast anything he don't want me to know about. One day massa was fit to be tied, he was in such a bad mood. Was ravin' about the crops, and taxes, and the triflin' niggers he got to feed. "Gonna sell 'em I swear fo' Christ, I'm gonna sell 'em," he says. Then ol' missus ask which ones he gonna sell and tell him quick to spell it. Then he spell out G-A-B-E and R-U-F-U-S. Course I stood there without batting any eye and making believe I didn't even hear him, but I was packing them letters up in my head all the time. And soon's I finished dishes I rushed down to my father and say 'em to him just like massa say 'em. Father say quietlike, "Gabe and Rufus," and told me to go on back to the house and say I ain't been out. The next day Gabe and Rufus was gone—they had run away. Massa nearly died. Got to cussin' and ravin' so, he took sick. Missus went to town and told the sheriff, but they never could find those two slaves.

SUSAN BROADDUS
The Negro in Virginia, p. 44.

· 3 ·

One of the more fascinating recorded stories of one who could be considered a "good" slave is the story of Josiah Henson. He was born a slave and grew up believing that while slavery was wrong, as a slave he had a responsibility to do his best work. During his early life he constantly courted his owner's favor.

At fifteen years of age there were few who could compete with me in work or sport. I was as lively as a young buck and running over with animal spirits. I could run faster, wrestle better, and jump higher than anybody about me, and at an evening shakedown in our own or a neighbor's kitchen, my feet became absolutely invisible from the rate at which they moved. All this caused my master and my fellow slaves to look upon me as a wonderfully smart fellow and prophesy the great things I should do when I became a man. My vanity became vastly inflamed and I fully coincided in their opinion. Julius Caesar never aspired and plotted for the imperial crown more ambitiously than did I to out-hoe, out-reap, out-husk, out-dance, out-everything every competitor; and from all I can learn he never enjoyed his triumph half as much. One word of commendation from the petty despot who ruled over us would set me up for a month.

Henson, pp. 18–19.

Henson eventually raised himself to be superintendent of the farm work and then overseer. In actual fact, he ran the entire plantation and his owner collected the profit. Yet Henson was proud of himself and proud to be able to provide such valuable service to his owner.

I retained . . . the especial favor of my master, who was not displeased either with saving the expense of a large salary for a white superintendent, or with the superior crops I was able to raise for him. I will not deny that I used his property more freely than he would have done himself in supplying his people with better food; but if I cheated him in this way, in small matters, it was unequivocally for his own benefit in more important ones, and I accounted with the strictest honesty for every dollar I received in the sale of the property entrusted to me. . . . It was my duty to be faithful to him in the position in which he placed me, and, I can boldly declare, before God and man, that I was so. I forgave him the causeless blows and injuries he had inflicted on me in childhood and youth and was proud of the favor he now showed me and of the character and reputation I had earned by strenuous and persevering efforts.

Henson, pp. 40–41.

Despite Henson's skillful management of the plantation, the owner dissipated the profits and eventually found himself in the position where all of his slaves were going to be auctioned off to pay his debts. He came to Henson and asked him to take all the slaves to Kentucky, where he had a brother. He would follow in a few months. It was remarkable that a white slave owner would ask a black slave to be responsible for other slaves on a journey of a thousand miles. It was even more remarkable that Henson discharged the responsibility.

My heart was aroused in view of the importance of my responsibility, and, heart and soul I became identified with my master's project of running off his negroes.

But a crisis developed while going down the Ohio River.

On passing along the Ohio shore, we were repeatedly told by persons conversing with us that we were no longer slaves but free men, if we chose to be so. At Cincinnati, especially, crowds of colored people gathered round us and insisted on our remaining with them. They told us we were fools to think of going on and surrendering ourselves up to a new owner; that now we could be our own masters and put ourselves out of all reach of pursuit. I saw the people under me were getting much excited. Divided counsels and signs of insubordination began to manifest themselves. I began, too, to feel my own resolution giving way. Freedom had ever been an object of my ambition, though no other means of obtaining it had occurred to me but purchasing myself. I had never dreamed of running away. I had a sentiment of honor on the subject. The duties of the slave to his master as appointed over him in the Lord, I had ever heard urged by ministers and religious men. It seemed like outright stealing. . . . Strange as it may seem, I really felt it then. Entrancing as the idea was that the coast was clear for a run for freedom, that I might liberate my companions, might carry off my wife and children and someday own a house and land and be no longer despised and abused—still my notions of right were against it. I had promised my master to take his property to Kentucky and deposit it with his brother Amos. Pride, too, came in to confirm me. I had undertaken a great thing; my vanity had been flattered all along the road by hearing myself praised; I thought it would be a feather in my cap to carry it through thoroughly, and had often painted the scene in my imagination of the final surrender of my charge to Master Amos, and the immense admiration and respect with which he would regard me. Under the influence of these impressions and seeing that the allurements of the crowd were producing a manifest effect, I sternly assumed the captain, and ordered the boat to be pushed off into the stream. A shower of curses followed me from the shore; but the negroes under me, accustomed to obey, and alas! too degraded and ignorant of the advantages of liberty to know what they were forfeiting, offered no resistance to my command.

Henson, pp. 50–52.

It should be added, however, that Henson goes on to say, "My soul [has] been pierced with bitter anguish at the thought of having been thus instrumental in consigning to the infernal bondage of slavery so many of my fellow-beings." And most significantly: "I knew not that the title deed of the slave owner is robbery and outrage."

Josiah Henson was one who totally accepted the slave owner's point of view. When he first began to realize that he should be free, he thought that the only correct manner of getting that freedom was to buy himself. He so accepted the slave owner's ideas that he equated running away with stealing himself. Eventually

Henson did make up his mind that it was all right to "steal" himself, and he escaped to Canada with his family. This did not occur, however, until after he had purchased his freedom, and his master had not only not freed him but had tried to sell him to another slave owner. Henson did redeem himself, however, by returning south twice to lead slaves out, and he was further instrumental in bringing 118 slaves to Canada.

· 4 ·

The field slaves were not exposed to the slave owner's ideas as much as the house servant. They had little contact with the slave owner, and many of them lived and died without having once set foot inside the slave owner's house. Thus the field slaves were able to create their own world within the plantation world, and from it they waged an everyday struggle against their enslavement.

Their interests were simple: to do as little work as possible and get as few whippings as possible. While this was never possible on a large scale, they had various tricks which they used to make the slave owner's life a little less than easy.

The most common was to appear to be the dumb, stupid animal that he knew his owner thought he was. It was to his advantage to appear ignorant, and the more ignorant he appeared to be, the less work he would have to do. Any sloppy work that he did would be *accepted as all that he was capable of doing. The field slave took advantage of his alleged inferiority.*

One prominent southern physician, Dr. Samuel W. Cartwright of the University of Louisiana, was so taken in by the slave's duplicity that he wrote a lengthy essay describing various diseases that were "peculiar to the Negro." The descriptions are good indications of the ways in which the slaves fought against their enslavement.

DYAESTHESIA AETHIOPICA: From the careless movements of the individuals affected with this complaint they are apt to do much mischief, which appears as if intentional, but is mostly owing to the stupidity of mind and insensibility of the nerves induced by the disease. Thus they break, waste, and destroy everything they handle; abuse horses and cattle; tear, burn, or rend their own clothing. . . . They wander about at night, and keep in a half nodding state by day. They slight their work—cut up corn, cane, cotton, and tobacco, when hoeing it. . . . They raise disturbances with their overseers. . . . When driven to labor by the compulsive power of the white man, he performs the task assigned to him in a headlong, careless manner, treading down with his feet or cutting with his hoe the plants he is put to cultivate; breaking the tools he works with, and spoiling everything he touches that can be injured by careless handling. Hence the overseers call it "rascality," supposing that the mischief is intentionally done.

Olmstead, p. 192.

The overseers called it "rascality." More accurately, it could be called sabotage. It was deliberate on the part of the slaves, for it was obvious to them that their lives did not change if there was a good cotton crop or a bad one. If they worked hard, they remained slaves. If they sabotaged the plantation work as much as possible, they remained slaves. And the latter was easier and more enjoyable.

"The women on a plantation," said one extensive Virginian slave owner to me, "will hardly earn their salt, after they come to the breeding age: they don't come to the field and you go to the quarters and ask the old nurse what's the matter and she says, 'Oh, she's not well, Master; she's not fit to work, sir'; and what can you do? You have to take her word for it that something or other is the matter with her; and you dare not set her to work; and so she lays up till she feels like taking the air again, and plays the lady at your expense."

Olmstead, p. 190.

One Mississippi slave convinced his master that he was nearly blind and therefore unfit to work. After the Civil War, he was freed, and once free, he proceeded to become one of the best farmers in the area, freedom having miraculously restored his sight.

This kind of sabotage did not measurably ease the lives of the slaves, however. The whip flew as often. The overseer's horn blew at every dawn. It was not

*the kind of sabotage that could have overthrown slavery,
but it did undermine it considerably. Most important,
it gave the slaves a decided feeling that they were men
and women.*

*Of course, the slaves' stratagem only succeeded as long
as the slave owner could not prove that the work was
being deliberately sabotaged. While the slaves may have
been tempted to let the master know that they were,
in many respects, the masters of those who held them
captive, they could not do so. They developed their abili-
ties to be who they weren't to a fine art and described it
in a song: "Got one mind for the boss to see; Got another
mind for what I know is me." They created among themselves a way of life that was different from the one the
slave owner wanted them to have. And everything the
slave owners taught them they learned in a way he hadn't
intended.*

I was never acquainted with a slave who believed that he
violated any rule of morality by appropriating to himself
anything that belonged to his master, if it was necessary
to his comfort. The master might call it theft and brand
it with the name of crime; but the slave reasoned differently
when he took a portion of his master's goods to satisfy his
hunger, keep himself warm, or to gratify his passion for
luxurious enjoyment.

Ball, p. 257.

A housemaid who had the reputation of being especially

devout was suspected by her mistress of having stolen from her bureau several trinkets. She was charged with the theft, and vociferously denied it. She was watched and the articles discovered openly displayed on her person as she went to church. She still, on her return, denied having them—was searched and they were found in her pockets. When reproached by her mistress and lectured on the wickedness of lying and stealing, she replied with the confident air of knowing the ground she stood upon, ". . . don't say I'm wicked . . . it's all right for us poor colored people to appropriate whatever of the white folks' blessings the Lord puts in our way."

Olmstead, p. 117.

The slave determined right and wrong very easily. Whatever the slave owner considered right, was wrong. Whatever he considered wrong, was right. For the slave, it was only considered stealing if you took something from a fellow slave. To take from the slave owner was merely to appropriate that which was, in actuality, yours. It was only through your labor that the slave owner acquired what he had.

· 5 ·

From the laws and physical force that the slave owners used to maintain slavery, it is obvious that the slaves did not become the puppets their owners would have liked. Laws were made governing every aspect of a slave's life, giving the slave no legal rights and the slave owner all.

These laws gave the slave owners control over the bodies of their "property," but the slave's mind remained in his possession. And to a certain degree, so did his body.

Even though the slaves returned from the fields exhausted at night, they would often sneak off to the woods for church services, singing, and parties, where they would sing and dance away the pain of the day and feel that ecstasy which comes from knowing that one is a human being, not a work animal.

White men were hired to patrol the roads and woods surrounding the plantations to catch any slave who might be going to a gathering or trying to escape. These "paddyrollers," as they were called by the slaves, had permission to whip any slave they caught.

When the niggers go round singing "Steal Away to Jesus" that mean there going to be a religious meeting that night. The masters before and after freedom didn't like them religious meetings, so us naturally slips off at night, down in the bottoms or somewheres. Sometimes us sing and pray all night.

ANONYMOUS
Library of Congress

I remember one night the paddyrollers come when we was having a big meeting in one of the cabins. They had a big wooden log stuffed with mud in the fire. That make a lot of hot coals to use. Just as we heard 'em, ol' man Jack Diggs and Charlie Dowal shoveled fire and coals right out the door on them devils. They ran from the fire and we ran from them. Ain't nobody get caught that time.

BETTY JONES
The Negro in Virginia, pp. 146–147.

I remember once when we was gonna have a meeting down in the woods near the river. Well, they made me the look-out boy and when the paddyrollers come down the lane past the church—you see they was expecting that the nig-gers gonna hold a meeting that night—well, sir, they tell me to step out from the woods and let 'em see me. Well, I does, and the paddyrollers that was on horseback come a-chasing after me, just a-galloping down the lane to beat the band. Well, I was just ahead of 'em and when they got almost up with me I just ducked into the woods. Course the paddyrollers couldn't stop so quick and kept on round the bed and then there came a-screamin' and cryin' that make you think that hell done bust loose. Them ol' paddy-rollers done rid plumb into a great line of grapevines that the slaves had stretched 'cross the path. And these vines tripped up the horses and throwed the ol' paddyrollers off in the bushes. And some done landed mighty hard, 'cause they was a-limpin' around and cussin' and callin' for the slaves to come and help them, but them slaves got plenty of sense. . . .

After that, ol' paddyrollers got wise and used to tie their horses and come creepin' through the woods on foot, until they find where this meeting was going on. Then they would rush in and start whipping and beating the slaves unmerciful. All this was done to keep you from serving God and do you know some of them devils was mean and sinful enough to say, "If I catch you here servin' God, I'll beat you. You ain't got no time to serve God. We bought you to serve us."

WEST TURNER
The Negro in Virginia, p. 146.

One anonymous slave recalled two verses of a song the slaves used to sing about the paddyrollers.

> Run, nigger, run,
> The paddyroll get you!
> Run, nigger, run,
> The paddyroll come!
>
> Watch, nigger, watch,
> The paddyroll trick you!
> Watch, nigger, watch,
> He got a big gun.

That was one of the songs the slaves all knowed. Sometimes I wonder if the white man didn't make that song up so us niggers would keep in line.

ANONYMOUS
Library of Congress

Generally the slaves only went out on Saturday nights, because they didn't have to rise to the sound of the overseer's horn on Sunday.

Massa Fleming ain't cared how much we dance, but ol' overseer would raise the devil. Overseer always said a slave never would work after he done dance all night. Used to complain to massa and he threaten not to let us dance if we didn't do our work but he never did stop us. Had to dance or do something. Work in the field all day and got to have some fun on Saturday nights.

HENRIETTA PERRY
The Negro in Virginia, p. 92.

Saturday nights we'd slip out the quarters and go to the woods. Was an ol' cabin 'bout five miles away from the house and us would raise all the ruckus there we wanted to. Used to dance ol' Jenny down. Who was Jenny? Wasn't nobody but me, I reckon. That's what we gals used to say. Gonna set the flo' with Jenny tonight. Sometimes we would say when missus was around, "Going to see Jenny tonight." And that mean us gonna have a dance, but missus didn't know what we talkin' about. Sometimes the boys say it too —can't tell you what they mean.
Anyhow, we'd go to these dances. Every gal with her beau and such music! Had two fiddles, two tangerines, two banjos and two sets of bones. Was a boy named Joe that used to whistle, too. Them devilish boys would get out in the middle of the flo' and me, Jenny and the devil right

with 'em. Set a glass of water on my head and the boys would bet on it. I had a great big wreath round my head an' a big ribbon bow on each side, and didn't waste a drop of water on none of 'em. . . .

BETTY JONES
The Negro in Virginia, p. 93.

We had parties and we'd sing:

> Massa sleeps in the feather bed,
> Nigger sleeps on the floor;
> When we get to heaven
> There'll be no slaves no more.

Then we had the song about this:

> Rabbit in the briar patch,
> Squirrel in the tree,
> Wish I could go hunting
> But I ain't free.
>
> Rooster's in the henhouse,
> Hen's in the patch.
> Love to go shooting,
> But I ain't free.

MILLIE WILLIAMS
Library of Congress

Saturday only worked half-day, and them slaves would sho' carry on 'cause was gonna celebrate that night. Ol' Charlie Snipes was the lead man, and he was the biggest cut-up in the quarters. We'd all be hoeing potatoes 'long behindst Charlie and he would be prancing and singing tunes for

us to chop by. This the song Charlie use to sing on
Saturdays.

> Going to the ball
> Feet de de diddle
> Whose going to the ball?
> Feet de de diddle
> Going to wear a red gown
> Feet de de diddle
> Wear a red gown
> Feet de de diddle
> Going to wear a velvet coat
> Feet de de diddle . . .

And keep it up, putting in words and kicking the clods in
step. And sometimes they take it up all over the field, just
a feet de de diddleing and stepping high and chopping
right in tune. Ol' overseer was name Barnes and he would
yell and cuss and lash the slaves near him with his cow-
hide, but he couldn't stop all them slaves from feeling
good, 'cause they gonna "set the flo' " that night.

GEORGIANNA GIBBS
The Negro in Virginia, p. 65–66.

Used to go over the Saunders place for dancing. Must've
been hundred slaves over there, and they always had the
best dances. Most times for the dance they had Dennis to
play the banjo. Dennis had a twisted arm, and he couldn't
do much work, but he sho' could pick that banjo. Gals

would put on they spare dress if they had one, and men would put a clean shirt on. Gals always tried to fix up for partyin', even if they ain't got nothin' but a piece of ribbon to tie in they hair. Most times wear your shoes to the dance and then take 'em off. Them ol' hard shoes make too much noise, and hurt your feet. Couldn't do no steppin' in the field shoes. . . .

What kind of dances? Well, they wasn't no special name to 'em. There was cuttin' the pigeon wings—that was flippin' your arms and legs round and holdin' your neck stiff like a bird do. Then there was going to the east, and going to the west—that was with partners and sometimes they got to kiss each other, but they stand back and kiss without wrappin' no arms round like the young folks do today. And there was calling the figures and that meant that the fiddler would call the number and all the couples got to cut that number.

Set the flo'? That was—well the couples would do that in turn. They come up and bend over toward each other at the waist, and the woman put her hands on her hips and the man roll his eyes all round and grin and they pat the flo' with they feet just like they was putting it in place. Used to do that best on dirt flo' so the feet could slap down hard against it. Sometimes they would set the flo' alone— either a man or a woman. Then they would set a glass of water on their head and see how many kinds of steps they could make without spilling the water.

Dancing on the spot was the same thing as set the flo'—

almost. Just mean you got to stay in the circle. The fiddler would take a charred corncob and draw a circle on the flo', then call one after the other up and dance in the circle. If your feet touch the edge you is out. That was just like a cakewalk, 'cause sometime they bake a cake and give it to the one that did the most steps on the spot. No, I never did win no cake, but I was pretty good at it just the same, I reckon.

FANNIE BERRY
The Negro in Virginia, pp. 92–93.

The biggest parties were held, however, at Christmas. There were certain holidays that were celebrated on most plantations—Good Friday, Independence Day, and at the end of cotton-chopping season. Christmas, however, was the biggest celebration. Discipline was eased considerably and the slaves were given two or three days off, and sometimes they got the entire week between Christmas and New Year.

Slaves lived just for Christmas to come round. Start getting ready the first snowfall. Commence to saving nuts and apples, fixing up party clothes, stitching lace and beads from the big house. General celebrating time, you see, 'cause husbands is coming home and families is getting united again. Husbands hurry on home to see their new babies. Everybody happy. Massa always send a keg of whiskey down to the quarters by ol' Uncle Silas, the house man. Ol' Joe would drink all he can long the way, but

there would be plenty for all. If that don't last, ol' Massa
Shelton gonna bring some more down himself.

FANNIE BERRY
The Negro in Virginia, p. 87.

*The slaves enjoyed Christmas, but it was soon over.
Once it was, the plantation returned to normal.*

True it was, indeed, that the fun and freedom of Christmas,
at which time my master relaxed his front, was generally
followed up by a portentous back-action, under which he
drove and cursed worse than ever; still the fun and freedom were fixed facts; we had had them and he could not
help it.

Henson, p. 20.

*The prayer meetings, the parties, and the holidays
did not make being a slave pleasurable. Nothing could
do that, but whatever pleasure the slave was able to
provide for himself was a remarkable testimony to the
ability to retain humanity under the most inhuman
conditions.*

· 6 ·

*One of the more constant tools that the slaves used
to resist the spiritual brutality of slavery was music.
In Africa music is not an art form as much as it is a
means of communication. It was the same for the*

descendants of Africa. Quite often the words of a song are meaningless and are used only because of their tonal and rhythmic value. The music of Africa is highly improvisational and a song is rarely sung twice in the same way. The slaves did not lose this improvisational ability when they fused their musical heritage with the Western music they found in America.

Songs were used in every aspect of their lives. They sang to ease the burden of work. They sang for dancing. They brought several African instruments to this country—notably the banjo—and made others when they got here. They used music as a means of expressing their joys and they could make music with practically anything that was available.

There wasn't no music instruments. Us take pieces of sheep's rib or cow's jaw or a piece of iron, with a old kettle, or a hollow gourd and some horsehairs to make the drum. Sometimes they'd get a piece of tree trunk and hollow it out and stretch a goat's or sheep's skin over it for the drum. They'd be one to four foot high and a foot up to six foot across. In general two niggers play with the fingers or sticks on this drum. Never seen so many in Texas, but they made some. They'd take the buffalo horn and scrape it out to make the flute. That sho' be heard a long ways off. Then they'd take a mule's jawbone and rattle the stick across its teeth. They'd take a barrel and stretch a ox's hide across one end and a man sat astride the barrel and beat on that hide with his hands and his feet and if he get to feel the music in his bones, he'd beat on that barrel with his head. Another man beat on wooden sides with sticks.

WASH WILSON
Library of Congress

Sing! I say they did sing. Sing about the cooking and about the milking and sing in the field.

HANNAH HANCOCK
Library of Congress

Mother was let off some days at noon to get ready for spinning that evening. She had to portion out the cotton they was gonna spin and see that each got a fair share. When mother was going round counting the cards each had spun she would sing this song:

> Keep your eye on the sun
> See how she run.
> Don't let her catch you with your work undone.
> I'm a trouble, I'm a trouble.
> Trouble don't last always.

That made the women all speed up so they could finish before dark catch 'em, 'cause it be mighty hard handlin' that cotton thread by firelight.

BOB ELLIS
The Negro in Virginia, p. 65.

Through the songs, they described slavery as it was.

We raise the wheat,
They give us the corn;
We bake the bread,
They give us the crust;
We sift the meal,
They give us the skin,
And that's the way
They take us in.
We skim the pot,
They give us the liquor,
And say that's good enough for the nigger.

The big bee flies high,
The little bee makes the honey.
The black folks make the cotton
And the white folks get the money.

Through the songs, they made fun of the slave owners.

One day Charlie saw ol' massa comin' home with a keg of whiskey on his mule. Cuttin' across the plowed field, the ol' mule slipped and massa come tumblin' off. Massa didn't know Charlie saw him and Charlie didn't say nothin'. But soon after a visitor come and massa called Charlie to the house to show off what he knew. Massa say, "Come here, Charlie, and sing some rhymes for Mr. Henson." "Don't know no new ones, Massa," Charlie answered. "Come on, you black rascal, give me a rhyme for my company—one he ain't heard." So Charlie say, "All right, Massa, I give you a new one if you promise not to whup me." Massa

promised, and then Charlie sung the rhyme he done made
up in his head 'bout massa.

> Jackass rared
> Jackass pitched
> Throwed ol' massa in the ditch.

Well, massa got mad as a hornet, but he didn't whup
Charlie not that time anyway. And don't you know us used
to set the flo' to that song? Mind you, never would sing
it when massa was round, but when he wasn't we'd swing
all round the cabin singing about how ol' massa fell off
the mule's back. Charlie had a bunch of verses:

> Jackass stamped
> Jackass humped
> Massa hear slave, you sho' get whupped.

JULIA FRASIER
The Negro in Virginia, pp. 94–95.

*The slave owners did all that they knew to break the
spirit of the black slaves. They failed because of black
resistance to their designs.*

Slavery did its best to make me wretched; I feel no particular obligation to it, but nature, or the blessed God of
youth and joy, was mightier than slavery. Along with
memories of miry cabins, frosted feet, weary toil under
the blazing sun, curses, and blows, there flock in others,
of jolly Christmas times, dances before old massa's door

for the first drink of eggnog, extra meat at holiday times, midnight visits to apple orchards, broiling stray chickens, and first-rate tricks to dodge work. The God who makes the pup gambol, and the kitten play, and the bird sing, and the fish leap, was the author in me of many a light-hearted hour.

Henson, pp. 20–21.

RESISTANCE TO
SLAVERY—2

*The slave owner lived in a fear that was almost as
bad as the fears held by the slaves. He had to live with
the knowledge that at any moment his slaves might try
to kill him. He knew, whether he admitted it to himself
or not, that if he had been held as a slave, he would
have done anything to gain his freedom. He knew, also,
that his own slaves had such thoughts. The record of
planned slave insurrections is long and it was mainly
due to treacherous house servants that most of these
planned uprisings were uncovered. And in one instance,
at least, the organizer of a slave insurrection betrayed
it.*

The year before my arrival in the country there was a
concerted movement among a number of slaves on Bayou
Bœuf, that terminated tragically indeed. . . . Lew Cheney
. . . conceived the project of organizing a company sufficiently strong to fight their way against all opposition, to
the neighboring territory of Mexico.

A remote spot, far within the depths of the swamp back of Hawkins' plantation, was selected as the rallying point. Lew flitted from one plantation to another, in the dead of night, preaching a crusade to Mexico, and creating a furor of excitement wherever he appeared. At length a large number of runaways were assembled; stolen mules, and corn gathered from the fields, and bacon filched from smokehouses had been conveyed into the woods. The expedition was about ready to proceed, when their hiding place was discovered. Lew Cheney, becoming convinced of the ultimate failure of his project, in order to curry favor with his master, and avoid the consequences which he foresaw would follow, deliberately determined to sacrifice all his companions. Departing secretly from the encampment, he proclaimed among the planters the numbers collected in the swamp, and, instead of stating truly the object they had in view, asserted their intention was to emerge from their seclusion the first favorable opportunity, and murder every white person along the bayou. . . . The fugitives were surrounded and taken prisoners, carried in chains to Alexandria, and hung by the populace. Not only those, but many who were suspected, though entirely innocent, were taken from the field and from the cabin, and without the shadow of process or form of trial, hurried to the scaffold. . . . Lew Cheney escaped, and was even rewarded for his treachery. He is still living, but his name is despised and execrated by all his race throughout the parishes of Rapides and Avoyelles.

Northup, pp. 247–248.

The inevitable white response to any mention of a slave insurrection was to institute even more force upon the slaves. In 1831, a Virginia slave named Nat Turner led an insurrection in which more than sixty whites were killed. Federal militia was eventually called in to stop the rebellion, and for a long time after, slaves throughout the South lived through a reign of terror.

Yet no matter how repressive slave owners became, there were always slaves who tried to escape, who knew little more than that if they followed the North Star they would eventually reach a place where they would be free. And they were always helped along their way by other slaves.

I heard a rap—bump! bump! on my door. I answered a-hollerin'! Then someone whispered, "Hush! Don't say nothing, but let me in!" I let her in. Lawd, that woman was all out of breath and a-begging. "Can I stay here tonight?" I told her she could, so the woman done sleep right there behind me in my bed all night. I knew she had run away, and I was gonna do my part to help her along. I took and heard the horses and talking in the woods. Dogs just a-barking. I peeped out the window and saw white folks go by. I didn't move, I was so scared they was gonna come in the cabin and search for that po' woman. Next morning she stole out from there and I ain't never seen her no more.

JENNIE PATTERSON
The Negro in Virginia, p. 133.

Father's name was John Jones Littleton. Had a long thin nose like a white man, and had the loveliest white teeth and the prettiest mouth, but his back was a sight. It was scarred up and brittled from shoulder to shoulder. Father got beat up so much that after a while he ran away and lived in the woods. Used to slip back to the house Saturday nights and sometimes Sunday when he knew massa and missus done gone to meeting. Mama used to send John, my oldest brother, out to the woods with food for Father, and what he didn't get from us the Lord provided. Never did catch him, though ol' massa search real sharp. Father wasn't the only one hiding in the woods. There was his cousin, Gabriel, that was hiding and a man named Charlie. Niggers was too sharp for white folks. White folks was sharp, too, but not sharp enough to get by ol' Nat. Nat? I don't know who he was. Old folks used to say it all the time. The meanin' I guess is that the niggers could always outsmart the white folks.

CORNELIA CARNEY
The Negro in Virginia, pp. 127–128.

It was not uncommon for escaped slaves to hide out in the woods. Sometimes they did so for years. During the late eighteenth and early nineteenth centuries, many slaves ran away and lived with the Indians. Others escaped and created their own settlements.

While driving in a chaise from Portsmouth to Deep-River, I picked up on the road a jaded-looking negro, who

proved to be a very intelligent and good-natured fellow. . . . He told me that his name was Joseph, that he
belonged to a church in one of the inland counties, and
that he was hired out by the trustees of the church to his
present master. . . . He liked to "mind himself," as he
did in the swamps. . . .

The Dismal Swamps are noted places of refuge for runaway negroes. They were formerly peopled in this way
much more than at present; a systematic hunting of them
with dogs and guns having been made by individuals who
took it up as a business, about ten years ago. Children were
born, bred, lived and died there. Joseph Church told me
he had seen skeletons, and had helped to bury bodies
recently dead. There were people in the swamps still, he
thought, that were the children of runaways, and who had
been runaways themselves all their lives. . . .

Joseph said that they had huts in "back places," hidden
by bushes, and difficult of access; he had, apparently, been
himself quite intimate with them. . . .

I asked if they were ever shot. "Oh, yes," he said, "when
the hunters saw a runaway if he tried to get from them,
they would call out to him, that if he did not stop they
would shoot, and if he did not, they would shoot, and
sometimes kill him. *"But some of 'em would rather be shot
than be took, sir,"* he added, simply. [Italics in original]

Olmstead, pp. 159–160.

*Some would rather be killed. Some preferred to kill
themselves if they were faced with the possibility of*

*being captured or of having to return to their owners
if they found themselves hopelessly lost.*

This day, when I was three or four miles from home, in
a very solitary part of the swamps, I heard the sound of
bells similar to those which wagoners place on the shoulders
of their horses. At first the noise of bells of this kind, in
a place where they were so unexpected, alarmed me. . . .
I therefore crouched down upon the ground under cover
of a cluster of small bushes that were near me, and lay,
not free from disquietude, to await the near approach of
these mysterious bells.
. . . at length, I heard footsteps distinctly in the leaves,
which lay dry upon the ground. . . . A moment after, I
saw come from behind a large tree, the form of a brawny,
famished looking, black man, entirely naked, with his hair
matted and shaggy; his eyes wild and rolling; and bearing
over his head, something in the form of an arch, elevated
three feet above his hair, beneath the top of which were
suspended the bells, three in number whose sound had first
attracted my attention. Upon a closer examination of this
frightful figure, I perceived that it wore a collar of iron
about its neck, with a large padlock pendant from behind,
and carried in its hand a long staff, with an iron spear in
one end. . . . It slowly approached within ten paces of
me, and stood still. . . .
The black apparition moved past me, went to the water
and kneeled down. The forest re-echoed with the sound
of the bells, and their dreadful peals filled the deepest

recesses of the swamps, as their bearer drank the water of the pond. . . . At the sound of my voice . . . he sprang to his feet, and at a single bound, rushed mid-deep into the water, then turning, he besought me in a suppliant and piteous tone of voice to have mercy upon him and not carry him back to his master. . . .

Rising from the bushes, I now advanced to the waterside, and desired him to come out without fear, and to be assured that if I could render him any assistance, I would do it most cheerfully. As to carrying him back to his master, I was more ready to ask help to deliver me from my own than to give aid to anyone in forcing him back. . . .

My new friend now desired me to look at his back, which was seamed and ridged with scars of the whip and hickory, from the pole of his neck to the lower extremity of his spine. The natural color of the skin had disappeared, and was succeeded by a streaked and speckled appearance of dusky white and pale flesh color, scarcely any of the original black remaining.

He told me his name was Paul, that he was a native of Congo, in Africa, and had been a slave five years. . . . He had then been wandering in the woods more than three weeks, with no other subsistence than the land tortoises, frogs, and other reptiles that he had taken in the woods, and the aid of his spear. . . .

He informed me that he had first run away from his master more than two years ago after being whipped with long hickory switches until he fainted. That he concealed himself in a swamp at that time ten or fifteen miles from this place for more than six months, but was finally betrayed by a woman that he sometimes visited. . . .

I advised Paul to bear his misfortunes as well as he could until the next Sunday, when I would return and bring with me a file, and other things necessary to the removal of his fetters. . . .

On the following Sunday, having provided myself with a large file which I procured from the blacksmith's shop belonging to the plantation, I again repaired to the place at the side of the swamp, where I had first seen the figure of this ill-fated man.

. . . on arriving at the spot where I had left him, I saw no sign of any person. The remains of the fire that I had kindled were here, and it seemed that the fire had been kept up for several days by the quantity of ashes that lay in a heap, surrounded by numerous small brands. . . . I concluded that Paul had relieved himself of his irons and gone to seek concealment in some other place; or that his master had discovered his retreat and carried him back to the plantation.

Whilst standing at the ashes, I heard the croaking of ravens at some distance in the woods and immediately afterwards, a turkey buzzard passed over me pursued by an eagle, coming from the quarter in which I had just heard the ravens. . . . I therefore concluded that there was some dead animal in my neighborhood that had called all these ravenous fowls together. It might be that Paul had killed a cow by knocking her down with a pine knot and that he had removed his residence to this slaughtered animal. Curiosity was aroused in me and I proceeded to examine the woods. I had not advanced more than two hundred yards when I felt oppressed by a most sickening stench and saw the trees swarming with birds of prey, buzzards perched upon their branches, ravens sailing amongst their boughs, and clouds of carrion crows flitting about and poising themselves amongst their boughs in a stationary position. . . . Proceeding onward, I came in view of a large sassafras tree. . . . This sassafras tree had many low horizontal branches, attached to one of which I now saw the cause of so vast an assembly of the obscene fowls of the air. The lifeless body of the unhappy Paul hung suspended by a cord made of twisted hickory bark, passed in the form of a halter round the neck and firmly bound to the limb of the tree. It was manifest that he had climbed the tree, fastened the cord to the branch, and then sprung off. . . . The bells had preserved the corpse from being devoured; for whilst I looked at it, I observed a crow descended upon it and made a stroke at the face with its beak, but the motion that this gave to the bells caused them to rattle, and the bird took to flight.

Ball, pp. 277–287.

Many thousands of slaves escaped. Those thousands more who could not did what they could with what they had.

"Just come to tell you, Massa, that I've labored for you

for forty years now. And I done earned my keep. You can sell me, lash me, or kill me. I ain't caring which, but you can't make me work no more."

The slave owner was shocked, but after a pause, he said,

"All right, Jake. I'm retiring you, but for God's sake, don't say anything to the other niggers."

BEVERLY JONES
The Negro in Virginia, p. 63.

I used to be awfully high-tempered even when I was a boy. . . . In them days all the children were called little Mistress or little Marster and their parents used to tell me that I shouldn't hit or fight them. But every time they crossed me I jumped them. I just couldn't help it. . . . One Saturday morning little Missy was sleeping late. She did not have to go to school. Ol' Missy told me to go and make up her bed. I went in and she didn't want to get up so that I could make the bed. I told her then that it was late and that ol' Missy said for her to get up. Then she got mad, jumped up in the bed and said, "You black dog, get out of here. I'll get up when I get ready." With that she slapped me as hard as she could right in my face. I saw stars. As soon as I got back to myself, I swung at her and if she hadn't been so quick I would have almost killed her for I hit at her with my fist and with all the force I had. I was just about ready to jump up on the bed and choke the life out of her when ol' Missy happened in. . . .

ANONYMOUS
Fisk, pp. 105–106

Stories of slaves fighting and murdering slave owners and overseers in self-defense are not uncommon. Solomon Northup almost killed his owner after the latter had tried to kill him with an axe. Northup's explanation for the murder that he almost committed was simple: "Life is dear to every living thing; the worm that crawls upon the ground will struggle for it. At that moment it was dear to me, enslaved and treated as I was." Northup decided against killing his master only because he would have been hanged for it. This thought alone saved the life of many a white person in the South. The slaves talked and planned insurrections and it was only the realization that an insurrection would not succeed that stopped most at the talking stage.

More than once I have joined in serious consultation when the subject has been discussed, and there have been times when a word from me would have placed hundreds of my fellow-bondsmen in an attitude of defiance. Without arms or ammunition, or even with them, I saw such a step would result in certain defeat, disaster and death, and always raised my voice against it.

During the Mexican War I well remember the extravagant hopes that were excited. The news of victory filled the great house with rejoicing, but produced only sorrow and disappointment in the cabin. In my opinion—and I have had opportunity to know something of the feeling of which I speak—there are not fifty slaves on the shores of Bayou Bœuf, but would hail with unmeasured delight the approach of an invading army.

Northup, pp. 239–240.

It should never be thought that if the large majority of slaves had had the weapons that whites possessed, they would not have used them and used them effectively. They were only held as slaves because they did not have the necessary means to make themselves free.

They are deceived who flatter themselves that the ignorant and debased slave has no conception of the magnitude of his wrongs. They are deceived who imagine that he arises from his knees with back lacerated and bleeding, cherishing only a spirit of meekness and forgiveness. A day may come—it *will* come, if his prayer is heard—a terrible day of vengeance, when the master in his turn will cry in vain for mercy.

Northup, p. 249.

□ 6 □

EMANCIPATION

In April of 1861 the Civil War began, and almost
immediately slaves in the upper southern states of Virginia, Maryland, and Delaware began leaving to join
the northern army. At first they were disappointed.
President Abraham Lincoln was more intent upon preserving the Union than he was in freeing the slaves.
He had ordered all northern army commanders to
return escaped slaves to their owners. But however
many the Union Army returned, twice that number came
from another direction to take their place. As far as
the slaves were concerned, the "bluecoats," as they
called the northern army, had come to liberate them and
they weren't going to take no for an answer. Wherever
the troops went, the slaves came, and soon, orders or
no orders, army commanders put them to work as laborers
and cooks, for which they were paid wages.

Most slaves did not have to be convinced to leave

*"ol' massa." Others did, like the young boy in the
following narrative whose brother, Jeff, had escaped
and joined the "Yankees." Jeff then came back to get
his little brother.*

He said, "I am with the Yankees and I slipped off to come
and get you. I have been ducking and dodging for three
days trying to get here. I want to take you with me. Don't
be scared of the Yankees. And even if we should get killed,
it won't be much worse than staying here."
I was scared of the Yankees and especially the cavalry for
I had seen troops of horses go by and they looked so awful
and sounded like thunder. Too, Massa Bill had always told
me that the Yankees were mean and would kill all the
Negroes they could get their hands on. But after I heard
what Jeff said I made up my mind to go. I was still young,
less than twenty, I know.

*The young boy took some food from the big house
and met his brother in the woods and traveled until
nightfall. The next morning while they were cooking
breakfast, some northern soldiers came.*

. . . some Yankees came by on horses. All the men had
their helmets tied under their chins and the horses' hoofs
sounded like thunder as they went running down the road.
It nearly scared me to death and I started to run but Jeff
caught me and said, "Charlie, the Yankees won't hurt you.

Haven't I been with them nearly a year? They are fighting Mars' Bill and the other white folks. They don't want to do nothing to us. They will pay us for our work and if Mars' Bill tries to get us after we get among them he will get his foot into it. For they told me that I didn't have to ever go back to him unless I wanted to. . . ."

We got to the camp early the next morning, just as the Yankees were taking the Negroes out to work. There must have been about a thousand slaves, and they all had axes, going out to cut wood. One troop of cavalry went in front and another behind. This was to protect the slaves from the rebels. . . .

When we came in sight of the advance horsemen, two of them came riding real fast toward us, with pistols in their hands. I got scared and jumped behind a tree and wouldn't come out. They hollered to Jeff and said, "Halt! Who goes there?" Jeff threw up his hands and said, "A workman of the camp, Number 89." By this time one of them was upon me. He said, "Who are you?" I said, "I belong to Mars' Bill." "What do you want here then? Didn't your master treat you good?" I said, "Mars' Bill treated me all right, but I wanted to be free and I came with my brother over here to work." All the others had come up about this time and after talking a little while, they told me to fall in line with my brother and the rest of the workers.

ANONYMOUS
Fisk, pp. 112–116.

Eventually blacks were employed as fighting troops in the Union Army, and since so many of them had so recently escaped from slavery, they fought fiercely and well throughout the Civil War.

There were also blacks used on the side of the Confederacy. Most were taken along to battle by their masters to be body servants. Most slaves, however, remained on the plantations, for they were the South's agricultural labor force, and if the Confederate troops were going to eat and be clothed, the slaves had to remain on the plantation to do the work.

Freedom did not come to most of the slaves until the end of the war in 1865. The Emancipation Proclamation of 1863 only applied to those areas of the South under Union control, which was not much at that time. The President of the Confederacy, Jefferson Davis, thought so little of the Emancipation Proclamation that he issued his own proclamation, which stated that all black people in all northern states were to be considered slaves.

The slaves, however, knew nothing of the legal subtleties involved in presidential proclamations. As soon as they heard a rumor that they were declared free, they didn't wait for further confirmation. They freed themselves, whether their owners liked it or not.

I was a young gal, about ten years old, and we done heard that Lincoln gonna turn the niggers free. Ol' missus say there wasn't nothin' to it. Then a Yankee soldier told some-

one in Williamsburg that Lincoln done signed the 'Mancipation. Was wintertime and mighty cold that night, but everybody commenced getting ready to leave. Didn't care nothin' about missus—was going to the Union lines. And all that night the niggers danced and sang right out in the cold. Next morning at daybreak we all started out with blankets and clothes and pots and pans and chickens piled on our backs, 'cause missus said we couldn't take no horses or carts. And as the sun come up over the trees, the niggers started to singing:

> Sun, you be here and I'll be gone
> Sun, you be here and I'll be gone
> Sun, you be here and I'll be gone
> Bye, bye, don't grieve after me
> Won't give you my place, not for yours
> Bye, bye, don't grieve after me
> 'Cause you be here and I'll be gone.

SUSIE MELTON
The Negro in Virginia, pp. 210–211.

Granma used to tell this story to everybody that would listen, and I expect I heard it a hundred times. Granma say she was hired out to the Randolphs during the war. One day while she was weeding corn another slave, Mamie Tolliver, come up to her and whispered, "Sarah, they tell me that Massa Lincoln done set all us slaves free." Granma say, "Is that so?" and she dropped her hoe and run all the way to the Thacker's place—seven miles it was—and run to ol' missus and looked at her real hard. Then she yelled, "I'm free! Yes, I'm free! Ain't got to work for you no more. You can't put me in your pocket now!" Granma say Missus Thacker started boo-hooing and threw her apron over her face and run in the house. Granma knew it was true then.

BETTY JONES
The Negro in Virginia, p. 209.

Some slave owners moved to Texas with their slaves when it appeared that the South might lose the war. By moving to Texas they hoped that they might hold on to their slaves a while longer.

We wasn't there in Texas long when the soldiers marched in to tell us that we were free. Seems to me like it was on a Monday morning when they come in. Yes, it was a Monday. They went out to the field and told them they was free. Marched them out of the fields. They come a-shouting. I remembers one woman. She jumped on a barrel and she shouted. She jumped off and she shouted. She jumped back on again and shouted some more. She kept that up for a long time, just jumping on a barrel and back off again.

ANNA WOODS
Library of Congress

The news that they were free was the fulfillment of the dream they had taken to bed each night and risen with each morning. How many times they had tried to imagine what that moment would be like, and now it had come. Some found it hard to believe.

One day I was out milking the cows. Mr. Dave come down into the field and he had a paper in his hand. "Listen to me, Tom," he said. "Listen to what I read you." And he read from a paper all about how I was free. You can't tell how I felt. "You're joking me," I says. "No, I ain't," says he. "You're free." "No," says I, "it's a joke." "No," says he, "it's a law that I got to read this paper to you. Now listen while I read it again."

But still I wouldn't believe him. "Just go up to the house," says he, "and ask Mrs. Robinson. She'll tell you." So I went. "It's a joke," I says to her. "Did you ever know your master to tell you a lie?" she says. "No," says I, "I ain't." "Well," she says, "The war's over and you're free." By that time I thought maybe she was telling me what was right. "Miss Robinson," says I, "can I go over to see the Smiths?" They was a colored family that lived nearby. "Don't you understand," says she, "you're free. You don't have to ask me what you can do. Run along, child." And so I went. And do you know why I was a-going? I wanted to find out if they was free, too. I just couldn't take it all in. I couldn't believe we was all free alike.

Was I happy? You can take anything. No matter how good you treat it—it wants to be free. You can treat it good

and feed it good and give it everything it seems to want
—but if you open the cage—it's happy.

TOM ROBINSON
Library of Congress

*Most slaves, though, had no difficulty at all believing
the news when they heard it.*

The news come on a Thursday and all the slaves been
shoutin' and carryin' on till everybody was tired out. I
remember the first Sunday of freedom. We was all sittin'
around restin' and tryin' to think what freedom meant and
everybody was quiet and peaceful. All at once ol' Sister
Carrie who was near 'bout a hundred started into talking:

> Tain't no mo' sellin' today.
> Tain't no mo' hirin' today.
> Tain't no mo' pullin' off shirts today.
> It's stomp down freedom today.
> Stomp it down!

And when she says, "Stomp it down," all the slaves commence to shoutin' with her:

> Stomp down freedom today
> Stomp it down!
> Stomp down freedom today.

Wasn't no more peace that Sunday. Everybody started in
to sing and shout once more. First thing you know they

done made up music to Sister Carrie's stomp song and sang and shouted that song all the rest of the day. Child, that was one glorious time!

CHARLOTTE BROWN
The Negro in Virginia, p. 212.

I remember hearing my pa say that when somebody come and hollered, "You niggers is free at last," say he just dropped his hoe and said in a queer voice, "Thank God for that." It made ol' miss and ol' massa so sick till they stopped eating a week. Pa said ol' massa and ol' miss looked like their stomachs and guts had a lawsuit and their navel was called in for a witness, they was so sorry we was free.

ANNIE MAE WEATHERS
Library of Congress

Daddy was down to the creek. He jumped right in the water up to his neck. He was so happy he just kept on scoopin' up handfulls of water and dumpin' it on his head and yellin', "I'se free! I'se free! I'se free!"

LOUISA BOWES ROSE
The Negro in Virginia, p. 208.

Niggers shoutin' and clappin' hands and singin'! Chillun runnin' all over the place beatin' time and yellin'! Everybody happy. Sho' did some celebratin'. Run to the kitchen and shout in the window:

Mammy don't you cook no more.
You's free! You's free!

Run to the henhouse and shout:

> Rooster, don't you crow no more.
> You's free! You's free!

Go to the pigpen and tell the pig:

> Ol' pig, don't you grunt no more.
> You's free! You's free!

Tell the cows:

> Ol' cow, don't you give no more milk.
> You's free! You's free!

And some smart aleck boys sneaked up under Miss Sara Ann's window and shouted:

> Ain't got to slave no more.
> We's free! We's free!

FANNIE BERRY
The Negro in Virginia, p. 210.

The war was over and when the South surrendered to the North at Appomattox, it was appropriate that there were blacks present to watch the official end of the war and slavery.

General Lee tipped his hat first and then General Grant tipped hissen. General Lee got off his horse, and General Grant got off hissen. General Lee got on a new uniform with gold braid and lots of buttons, but General Grant got on an old blue coat that's so dirty it look black. They stood there talking about half an hour and then they shake hands and us what was watching know that Lee done give up. Then General Lee tipped his hat and General Grant tipped hissen, and General Lee rode over to the rebel side. General Grant rode over to our side and the war was over.

TOM HESTER
The Negro in Virginia, p. 204.

But with the end of the war, there were, of course, those slave owners who said nothing to their slaves about the war being over or that they were free.

Guess I was about fifteen years old when massa come back from the fighting, mean as ever. Never did say nothing about the war and I didn't even know if it's over or not. But one day Massa Bob, his son, was switchin' me in the woods playful-like and he say, "Why don't you strike me back, Mici? You's free. That's what the war was for, to free the niggers." I took that switch away and beat him hard as I could across the head till it busted. Then I run across the fields to some colored folks about six miles away. Their names was Foreman and they was free sho' 'nough. They told me that was right. I been free more than a year. Ain't never been back to that place.

ARMACIE ADAMS
The Negro in Virginia, p. 209.

Freedom. One day they had been awakened by the sound of the overseer's horn. The next day they were not. One morning they had gone to the fields and before the sun set, they had left their hoes, their plows, their cotton sacks lying in the furrows. And they put the full meaning of it into one eloquent phrase, which they sang over and over.

Free at last,
Free at last,
Thank God A-Mighty,
I'm free at last.

AFTER EMANCIPATION

The glorious feeling of freedom did not last long. Under slavery, the physical needs of the slaves had been supplied, however inadequately. With freedom they suddenly found themselves in a position where they had to supply their own needs. All were willing and able to do so, but to do so they required land of their own and farm equipment to get started. To be really free, it was necessary that they be able to make a living by themselves; it was necessary that they not have to go to those who had formerly held them slaves and ask for jobs.

There were some members of Congress who were aware of the problem. It was true, they argued, that Negroes could now vote, but the vote alone was not enough. Blacks had to be economically independent from a white South that was built on black slavery and resented black freedom. These congressmen, the Radical Republicans

as they were called, argued for "forty acres and a mule"
for every ex-slave. Their arguments were in vain. Free-
dom did not come to blacks. It merely visited for a
while.

The Yankee soldiers give out news of Freedom. They was
shouting around. I just stood around to see what they was
gonna do next. Didn't nobody give me nothing. I didn't
know what to do next. Didn't nobody give me nothing.
I didn't know what to do. Everything going. Tents all gone,
no place to stay and nothin' to eat. That was the big freedom to us colored folks. I got hungry and naked and cold
many a time. I had a good master and I thought he always
treated me heap better than that. I wanted to go back,
but I had no way.

JAKE GOODRIDGE
Library of Congress

It seem like it took a long time for freedom to come.
Everything just kept on like it was. We heard that lots of
slaves was getting land and some mules to set up for their
selves. I never knowed any what got land or mules nor
nothin'.

MITTIE FREEMAN
Library of Congress

Freedom turned into another kind of slavery, for
many slaves were forced to return to their former

plantations and ask "ol' massa" for a job. The former slave owners were happy, of course, to see the ex-slaves return, for the fields needed plowing and the crops planting. Instead of paying the ex-slaves wages, however, the former slave owners let them work on "shares." The plantation owner would provide them with cotton-seed, a house, food, farm tools. Once the crop was harvested, he would take half, plus enough crops to cover the cost of the seed, tools, rent, and food that he had let the ex-slave have. Once the owner had deducted his share and the expenses incurred, what was left was the ex-slave's "share." Usually that was nothing.

Then the next bad thing happened to us poor niggers after the war was this. The white folks would pay niggers to lie to the rest of the niggers to get the farming done for nothing. He'd tell us come on and go with me, a man wants a gang of niggers to do some work and he pay you like money growing on trees. Well, we ain't had no money and ain't use to none. So we glad to hear that good news. We just up and bundle up and go with this lying nigger. They carries us by the droves to different parts of Alabama, Arkansas and Missouri. After we got to these places they put us all to work all right on the great big farms. We all light in and work like old horses, thinking how we making money and going to get some of it, but we never did get a cent. We never did get out of debt. We always get through with fine big crops and owed the white man more than when we started the crop and got to stay to pay the debt. It was awful. All over was like that.

ULRICH EVANS
Library of Congress

Ol' miss and massa was not mean to us at all until after surrender and we were freed. We did not have a hard time until after we were freed. They got mad at us because we was free and they let us go without a crumb of anything and without a penny and nothing but what we had on our backs. We wandered around and around for a long time. Then they hired us to work on halves and man, we had a hard time then and I've been having a hard time ever since.

FRANK FIKES
Library of Congress

Slavery returned in almost every respect except name. Many slaves made plans in case slavery did return.

When us black folks got set free, us'n change our names, so effen the white folks get together and change their minds and don't let us be free any more, then they have a hard time finding us.

ALICE WILKINS
Library of Congress

The names didn't matter though. They were known by the color of their skin and they became objects to be kept in their place. A white terrorist group was organized right after the Civil War in 1866 called the Ku Klux Klan. The former slave trader and Confederate general, Nathan Bedford Forrest became the head of it, and it became one of the main instruments to keep blacks from possessing their freedom.

After us colored folks was considered free and turned loose, the Klu Klux broke out. Some colored people started to farming and gathered old stock. If they got so they made good money and had a good farm, the Klu Klux would come and murder 'em. The government builded schoolhouses and the Klu Klux went to work and burned 'em down. They'd go to the jails and take the colored men out and knock their brains out and break their necks and throw 'em in the river.

There was a colored man they taken. His name was Jim Freeman. They taken him and destroyed his stuff and him 'cause he was making some money. Hung him on a tree in his front yard, right in front of his cabin. . . .

PIERCE HARPER
Botkin, pp. 256–257.

I come in contact with the Klu Klux. Us left the plantation in '65 and by '68 us was having such a awful time with the Klu Klux. First time they come to my mama's house at midnight and claim they was soldiers done come back from the dead. They all dress up in sheets and make up like spirit. They groan roun' and say they been killed

wrongly and come back for justice. One man, he look just like an ordinary man, but he sprung up about eighteen feet high all of a sudden. Another say he so thirsty he ain't have no water since he been killed at Manassas Junction. He ask for water and he just kept pouring it in. Us think he sho' must be a spirit to drink that much water. Course, he not drinking it. He was pouring it in a bag under his sheet. My mama never did take up no truck with spirits, so she knowed it was just a man. They tell us what they going to do if we don't all go back to our masters. Us all agrees and then they all disappear.

ANONYMOUS
Library of Congress

When the Union Army left the South in 1876, after occupying it from the close of the Civil War, political power returned to the former slave owners. Almost immediately, state legislatures began passing laws restricting the movements and activities of blacks. These laws were little different from the laws that were on the books during slavery itself. But instead of calling it slavery, it was called segregation. It was inevitable from the moment the North refused to ensure the freedom of blacks which had been won with four years of bloody fighting.

Slaves prayed for freedom. When they got it, they didn't know what to do with it. They was turned out with nowhere to go and nothing to live on. They had no experience in looking out for themselves and nothing to work with and no land. They made me think of the crowd one time who prayed for rain when it was dry in crop time. The rain fell in torrents and kept falling till it was about a flood. The rain frogs begin to holler and calling more rain and it rained and rained. Then the rain crow got up in a high tree and he hollered and asked the Lord for rain. It rained till every little rack of cloud that come over brought a big shower of large drops. The fields was so wet and miry you could not go in 'em, and water was standing in the fields, middle of every row, while the ditches in the fields looked like little rivers, they was so full of water. It began to thunder again in the southwest, right where we call the "Chub Hole" of the sky, where so much rain comes from and the clouds grow blacker and blacker back there.

Then one of the men who had been praying for rain looked up and said, "I tell you, brothers, if it don't quit raining everything going to be washed away." They all looked at the black rain cloud in the west with sorrowful faces as if they felt they didn't know what use they had for rain after they got it. Then one of the brothers said to the other brothers kind of easy and shameful-like, "Brothers, don't you think we overdone this thing?" That's what many a slave thought about praying for freedom. Slavery was a bad thing and freedom of the kind we got with nothing to live on was bad.

Two snakes full of poison. One lying with his head pointing north, the other with his head pointing south. Their names was slavery and freedom. The snake called slavery lay with his head pointed south and the snake called freedom lay with his head pointed north. Both bit the nigger and they was both bad.

PATSY MICHENER
Library of Congress

EPILOGUE

The legacy of slavery has been bitter and in the 103 years since the end of the Civil War little has been done to alleviate the bitterness. Much of that bitterness was reflected in some of the interviews conducted by the Federal Writers' Project in the 1930's. Seventy years after the end of the Civil War, some ex-slaves expressed attitudes and feelings, which, if anyone had bothered to listen, once more gave the lie to the stereotype of the happy slave, of the slave freed by the Emancipation Proclamation and accepted as a man equal to any other.

I was setting here thinking the other night 'bout the talk of them kind of white folks going to Heaven. Lord God, they'd turn Heaven wrong side out and have the angels working to make them something they could take away from them.

JACK MADDOX
Library of Congress

I believe it would have been better to have moved all the colored people way out west to themselves. Abraham Lincoln wanted to do this. It would have been better on both races and they would not have mixed up. But the white people did not want the "shade" taken out of the country. Many of the bosses after the freedom couldn't stand it and went in the house and got a gun and blew out his brains. If Lincoln had lived, he would have separated us like they did the Indians. We would not have been slaughtered, burned, hanged, and killed if we had been put to ourselves and had our own laws. Many a person is now in torment because of this mixup. God give us a better principle and we could have had thousands of whites slaughtered, but we didn't after the freedom.

RHODY HOLSELL
Library of Congress

Lincoln got the praise for freeing us, but did he do it? He give us freedom without giving us any chance to live to ourselves and we still had to depend on the southern white man for work, food and clothing, and he held us out of necessity and want in a state of servitude but little better than slavery. Lincoln done but little for the Negro race and from a living standpoint, nothing. White folks are not going to do nothing for Negroes except keep them down. Harriet Beecher Stowe, the writer of *Uncle Tom's Cabin*, did that for her own good. She had her own interests at heart and I don't like her, Lincoln, or none of that crowd. The Yankees helped free us, so they say, but they let us be put back in slavery again.

When I think of slavery it makes me mad. I do not believe in giving you my story, 'cause with all the promises that have been made, the Negro is still in a bad way in the United States, no matter in what part he lives. It's all the same. Now you may be all right; there're a few white men who are, but the pressure is such from your white friends that you will be compelled to talk against us and give us the cold shoulder when you are around them, even if your heart is right towards us.

You are going around to get a story of slavery conditions and the persecutions of Negroes before the Civil War and the economic conditions concerning them since that war. You should have known before this late day all about that. Are you going to help us? No! You are only helping yourself. You say that my story may be put into a book, that you are from the Federal Writers' Project. Well, the Negro will not get anything out of it, no matter where you are from. Harriet Beecher Stowe wrote *Uncle Tom's Cabin.* I didn't like her book and I hate her. No matter where you are from I don't want you to write my story, 'cause the white folks have been and are now and always will be against the Negro.

THOMAS HALL
Library of Congress

About the Author

A frequent contributor to *The New Republic* and other journals, Julius Lester is the author of many highly acclaimed books including *This Strange New Feeling*, available as a Point paperback. He is also the author of *Long Journey Home* (a National Book Award finalist in 1972), *All Is Well: An Autobiography*, and *Do Lord Remember Me*. Mr. Lester is a professor of black studies at the University of Massachusetts in Amherst, where he lives with his wife, three children, and stepdaughter.

BIBLIOGRAPHY

Ball, Charles. *A Narrative of the Life and Adventures of Charles Ball, A Black Man,* 3rd ed. Pittsburgh: John T. Shryock, 1854.

Bennett, Lerone, Jr. *Before the Mayflower.* Baltimore: Penguin, Pelican Books, Inc., 1966.

Bontemps, Arna, and Hughes, Langston, eds. *The Book of Negro Folklore.* New York: Dodd, Mead & Company, 1959.

Botkin, B. A., ed. *Lay My Burden Down: A Folk History of Slavery.* Chicago: The University of Chicago Press, 1945.

Brown, William W. *Narrative of William W. Brown, A Fugitive Slave Written by Himself.* Boston: Bela Marsh, 1849.

Davidson, Basil. *The African Slave Trade.* Boston: Atlantic-Little, Brown, 1961.

Dennett, John Richard. *The South As It Is: 1865–1866.* New York: The Viking Press, Inc., 1967.

Evidence on the Slave Trade. Cincinnati: American Reform Tract and Book Society, 1855.

Federal Writers' Project. *The Negro in Virginia.* New York: Hastings House, 1940.

Fisk University. *God Struck Me Dead: Religious Conversion Experiences and Autobiographies of Negro Ex-Slaves.* Nashville, Tennessee: Fisk University Social Sciences Institute, 1945.

Franklin, John Hope. *From Slavery to Freedom.* 3rd ed. New York: Alfred A. Knopf, Inc., 1967.

Genovese, Eugene D. *The Political Economy of Slavery.* New York: Random House, Vintage Books, 1967.

Henson, Josiah. *Father Henson's Story of his own Life.* New York: Corinth Books, 1962.

Nichols, Charles H. *Many Thousand Gone: The Ex-Slaves' Account of Their Bondage and Freedom.* Leiden, Germany: E. J. Brill, 1963.

Northup, Solomon. *Twelve Years a Slave.* Buffalo: Miller, Orton & Mulligan, 1854.

Olmstead, Frederick. *Journey in the Seaboard Slave States.* New York: Dix & Edwards, 1856.

Stampp, Kenneth M. *The Peculiar Institution.* New York: Random House, Vintage Books, 1956.

Wade, Richard C. *Slavery in the Cities.* New York: Oxford University Press, Inc., 1964.

Weld, Theodore, ed. *American Slavery As It Is: Testimony of A Thousand Witnesses.* New York: American Anti-Slavery Society, 1839.

Wish, Harvey, ed. *Slavery in the South.* New York: Noonday Press, a division of Farrar, Straus and Giroux, Inc., 1964.